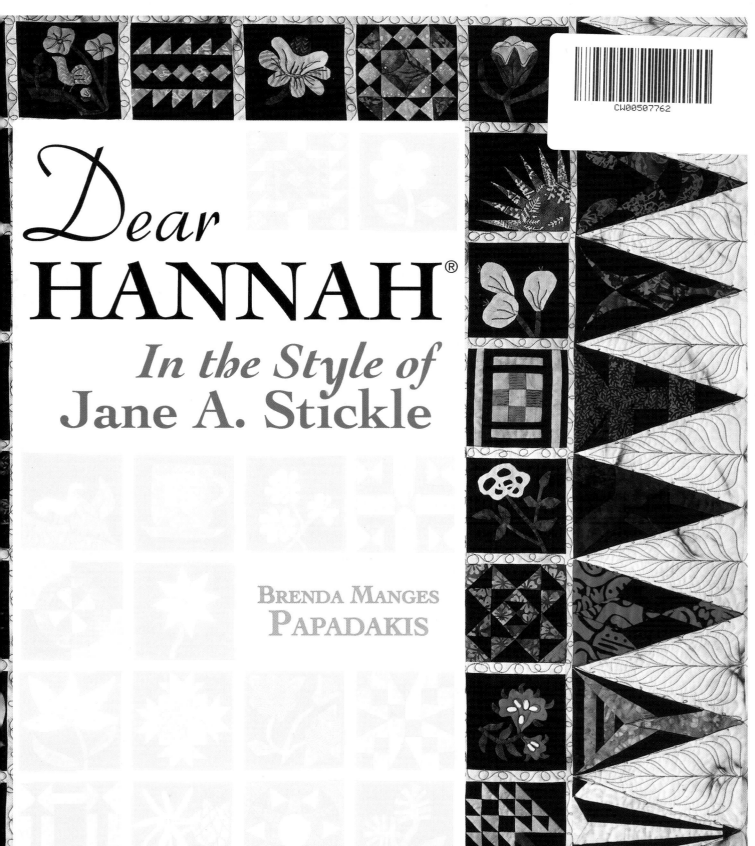

Dear HANNAH®

In the Style of
Jane A. Stickle

BRENDA MANGES
PAPADAKIS

Located in Paducah, Kentucky, the American Quilter's Society (AQS) is dedicated to promoting the accomplishments of today's quilters. Through its publications and events, AQS strives to honor today's quiltmakers and their work and to inspire future creativity and innovation in quiltmaking.

EDITOR: BARBARA SMITH
GRAPHIC DESIGN: LYNDA SMITH
COVER DESIGN: MICHAEL BUCKINGHAM
PHOTOGRAPHY: CHARLES R. LYNCH

Library of Congress Cataloging-in-Publication Data

Papadakis, Brenda Manges, 1943-
   Dear Hannah : in the style of Jane A. Stickle / by Brenda Manges Papadakis.
      p. cm.
    ISBN 1-57432-827-1
   1. Patchwork--Patterns. 2. Appliqué--Patterns. 3.
Quilting--Patterns. 4. Quilting History.   I. Title.

   TT835.P3514 2003
    746.46'041--dc21

                              2003013333

Additional copies of this book may be ordered from the American Quilter's Society, PO Box 3290, Paducah, KY 42002-3290, or online at www.AQSquilt.com.

Leona Gail Puckett

Dedication

Dear Hannah is dedicated to Leona Gail Puckett Stewart, a loving and trusted friend. She kept me focused on this project and was determined I would see it to fruition. No block or triangle was too great a challenge to her, and she hand-pieced most of MANY HANDS MAKE LIGHT WORK. Her advice is priceless. I treasure her friendship and every moment we spend together. Gail has taught a multitude of classes, and she is very active in promoting quilting.

This book is also dedicated to my grandchildren, and to all the other children of the world...our joy today and our hope for tomorrow.

In Loving Memory

Rebecca Jo Burnett Hamilton
August 30, 1952–April 19, 2002

A little lamb, a lock of hair,
A tiny quilt, a photo near
'Becca Jo, I sit and stare
Wishing you were here.

brenda lynn

Rebecca Jo Burnett Hamilton

Acknowledgments

Thank you, American Quilter's Society and Meredith Schroeder, for the invitation to write *Dear Hannah* and for the patience to wait for its completion. Thank you also, Barbara Smith, for editing and helping make this book a reality.

Dear Hannah is possible because of the contributions of so many Dear Jane Friends. It was written by your encouraging words, your quilts, your blocks, and your desire for more Jane blocks. To the guilds, shows, and quilt shops: thank you for giving me the opportunity to share my journey with Jane.

Thank you to all of the quilters who gave their talents and time helping with quilts for *Dear Hannah:*

Gail Stewart for hand-piecing a majority of the MANY HANDS QUILT.

Pam Austin for embroidering the appliqué blocks in GRANDMOTHER AND ME and for sharing your treasured relationship with your grandmother.

Kathleen Springer and Vickie Fallon for assembling GRANDMOTHER AND ME.

Edith Shanholt for making the top EDITH DARLENE.

DEAR HANNAH quiltmakers: Mary Althaus, Pam Austin, Tilde Binger, Gay Bomers, Connie Clark, Karan Flanscha, Susanne Kleen, Lu Ann Krug, Kathy Moak, Jennifer Perkins, Kathy Saunders, Diane Rode Schneck, Edith Shanholf, and Gail Stewart. *Dear Hannah* hooked rug by Sandra Kandris.

Quilters who made blocks for MANY HANDS MAKE LIGHT WORK: Claire Baker, Tilde Binger, Virginia Bohnenkamp, Irene Carrig, Val Champ, Mary Chester, Alice Curtis, Susanne Ellenberger, Vickie Fallon, Karan Flanscha, Elaine Frey, Carol Honderich, Rockie Ivins, Susanne Kleen, Marcie Knudson, Susan Kraftcheck, Jeanne Meddaugh, Teri Reymann, Ellie Schaefer, Diane Rode Schneck, Edith Shanholt, Marie Troyer, Jeane Tucker, and Nancy Zinni.

Judy Day in Australia and Vickie Fallo, Medford, New Jersey, for making the blocks in FRIENDS and to Virginia Bohnenkamp for hand quilting.

To all the Dear Janes in Europe who are teaching us just how small this world is becoming and for making the blocks in EUROPEAN JANE; to Joes Meester in Amsterdam for organizing the Holland Janes to make the Dear Jane blocks in EUROPEAN JANE; to Tilde Binger for organizing the European Dear Janes in making the Dear Hannah blocks for this quilt; to Claire Baker for assembling EUROPEAN JANE.

Richtje Beintema in Holland for permission to use her CIRCLE OF FRIENDS pattern.

Winners of the Dear Hannah Triangle Design Contest: Linda Franz, A HEROINE; Anna Holm, ANNA'S CAROUSEL; and Keri Schell, SUNRISE. A special thank you goes to my husband, Pete, for his original drawings of the other 45 triangle patterns.

Barb Vlack for drawing the World Without End and Mariner's Compass blocks for the corner kites in Electric Quilt™.

Block A–5, page 20.

Dean Neumann and Penny McMorris for their Electric Quilt programs that enable us to draw and design new quilts.

Amish friends Salome and Mary for hand quilting MANY HANDS MAKE LIGHT WORK and GRANDMA AND ME. A special thank you to Sue Ellenberger for coordinating the shipping and quilting of these two quilts.

Cathy Franks for machine quilting EDITH DARLENE, SARA ELEANORA, EUROPEAN JANES, DISTANT STAR.

To Richard Cleveland, Xenia Cord, Penny McMorris, and Mary Coyne Penders for sharing their knowledge about quilting in the twentieth century, especially after the 1950s and the Great Quilt Revival of the 1970s.

Art Henthorn for enriching my knowledge of the Enchanting Number Seven.

Rebecca Haarer for generously sharing her Amish heritage and quilts.

Brenda Roumie for providing wondrous organization and assistance in all aspects of my life and work.

Lou Allen Cox Bowling for loving me and teaching me what it means to be a "Mamaw."

Children: Maria Christina, Audrey Denise, Michael Duff, Jason Gerard; Aracely Reyes Bowling, daughter-in-law, and our own San Antonio Rose.

Grandchildren: Hannah Lou, Nathan Alexander, and Benjamin George whose hugs are the most precious gifts in the world.

Pete, husband, dearest friend, who knows me better than I know myself. Your contributions and encouragement make *Dear Hannah* very special. Thank you for loving me and sharing my life lo these many years.

Block J–1, page 84.

Block D–10, page 46.

Block J–5, page 87.

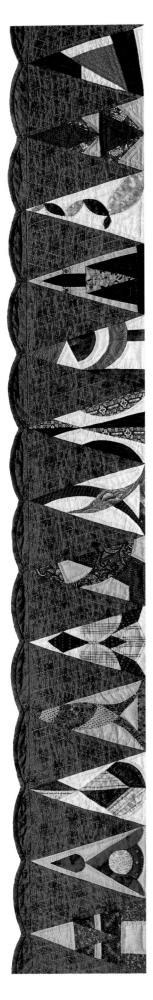

Contents

Letters to Hannah

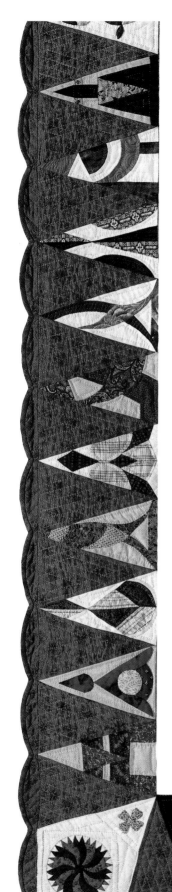

Introduction

The seeds of *Dear Hannah*® were planted with the birth of my granddaughter, Hannah, six months before the publication of my first book, *Dear Jane* (EZ Quilting by Wrights, 1996). The idea for *Dear Hannah* lay dormant until the first generation of "Janiacs" began finishing their Dear Jane quilts and began asking, "What are we going to do next?" That's when I started looking for another antique quilt to reproduce and pattern for them.

I found an appliqué quilt from 1850. I asked my husband, Pete, to draw the blocks, and I made patterns from his drawings. Then I found another quilt in the 1999 Cyril Nelson Quilt Calendar. It had Salinda Rupp's pieced quilt from 1870. This quilt fascinated me, and I started drafting some of its unique blocks.

During the years from 1996 to 1999, *Dear Jane* was growing and thriving and so was my little Hannah Lou. She needed a journal from me – I had found a writing project. In the spring of 2000, AQS invited me to write a sequel to *Dear Jane*®, and I happily accepted, thus the book *Dear Hannah* began.

For the DEAR HANNAH quilt, I decided to combine elements of the 1850 appliqué quilt with pieced blocks from Salinda Rupp's quilt. Wanting a smaller quilt than Jane Stickle's, I used an 11-by-13-block layout, for a total of 143 blocks. My friends, Gay Bomers and Rosemary Youngs, helped me select 72 blocks from the appliqué quilt. For the pieced blocks, I combined three dozen blocks from Salinda Rupp's quilt with some of my own favorites. The next design challenge was the layout.

Jane Stickle had used a Trip Around the World color setting, and I decided I would, too. Having drawn the layout of DEAR HANNAH in Electric Quilt, I was able to play with some different color placements for the blocks and chose to follow the color wheel in the setting.

Dear Hannah: In the Style of Jane A. Stickle – Brenda Manges Papadakis

While trying to decide every detail of the quilt – appliqué, piecing, placement, color – I asked my friend Gail Stewart, "Do you think this will ever be a quilt?" Beloved Gail said, "Of course, it will! How many blocks of each color do you need? Which are appliqué? Hand me some patterns and pull some fabric." This was the beginning of the quilt, Many Hands Make Light Work (photo on page 14).

For this quilt, I started with red in the center to give it a warm appearance. It was made to look traditional to represent the end of the nineteenth century. Another friend, Edith Shanholt, agreed to make the quilt, Edith Darlene (photo on page 19), from batiks to represent contemporary quilts from the end of the twentieth century. She started with a green circle-of-friends block in the center, and her finished quilt has a cool appearance.

The next puzzle to be solved in the evolution of Many Hands Make Light Work was the design of the triangle patterns for the border. While I was trying to decide how to proceed, engineer-artist Pete said to me, "Show me that computer drawing program you use." The next thing I knew, he had a dozen wonderful triangles. He asked, "How many do you want?" and I replied, "about 50." A little while later, there they were!

The letters to my granddaughter about the twentieth century are a natural follow-up to the letters in *Dear Jane* about life in the nineteenth century. Hannah needs to understand the events that defined that time. I also want her to know the continuing development of quilting. It is my hope that she will gain an insight into women's history and the female struggle for equality that continues even today. The letters are not to Hannah alone, but also to my grandchildren, Benjamin and Nathan, and to all of your children and grandchildren. I am fortunate to be able to write this book and tell my stories. Your stories are equally as important. Please write them down for your children and grandchildren, nieces, and nephews. Your journal is your greatest legacy!

Enjoy your journey!

Making Your Own *Dear Hannah*

Gather Your Supplies

In preparation for making your own DEAR HANNAH quilt, here are the supplies you will need to assemble.

Fabric

Selection

You may want to select a theme for your quilt. These blocks are beautiful in reproduction fabrics. They are also wonderful in Amish solids, 1930s reproductions, batiks, or jewel tones. Just look through the quilt photos. You will see an amazing variety to help you decide just how you want to make your quilt.

Amount

For hand-piecing and appliqué, you will need about eight yards of background fabric. If you are using two backgrounds, get four yards of each. For hand or machine-piecing, or for foundation piecing some of your blocks, you will need about 15 yards of background fabric. If you plan to use foundation piecing for most of your blocks, you will need about 20 yards.

Content

When I was learning to sew, my mother told me to buy only the very best fabrics I could afford. She

Block C–6, page 36.

would say, "The amount of time spent sewing a dress will be wasted if the fabric fades quickly or doesn't hang well." I still heed this advice when selecting quilt fabrics. I use only 100-percent cotton, and I recommend you do the same.

While talking about cotton, I must mention a little something about greige goods. (Greige is pronounced gray.) Greige goods are the raw unfinished fabrics. I know you've seen a print in a fabric chain store and then went to your quilt shop to see the very same print at almost twice the price. You're right – part of the difference is in the quality of the greige goods.

For us, the most useful characteristic of greige goods is thread count. The ideal thread count is 70 x 70; that is, in one square inch of fabric, 70 threads run across the weave and 70 threads run lengthwise. Only a couple of manufacturers use this thread count today. Most of the fabrics available to us in our quilt shops are about 62 x 62. Just for fun, take a swatch of fabric from your stash and check the thread count. The moral of this story is to be an informed buyer and purchase the best materials you can afford.

Preparation

There was a time when every piece of fabric I brought in the door was washed in heavy laundry detergent. Then I met Harriet Hargrave. Bowing to her wisdom, I now use only Orvus® soap and cold water on both my clothing and my quilts. Nothing has bled or faded. If you cannot find this product at your local quilt shop, try any farmers' cooperative in your area. It's actually horse shampoo. Horses have delicate skin and need a very mild shampoo. Never put fabrics in hot water because this may cause the dye to bleed.

If you don't pre-wash, then you must first test your fabrics, particularly reds. Fabrics that are likely to bleed or fade will often show color when rubbed with a tissue. With questionable fabrics, set a 3" swatch of each in a separate glass of warm water for about 10 minutes, then place the swatches on a piece of the lightest fabric in your quilt. If bleeding occurs, don't use the fabric.

Notions

Cutting Mats

To cut strips for machine-piecing, I use a large Olfa® mat. For trimming or cutting individual pieces, I place a 5" x 7" Olfa mat on the large mat, so I can easily turn the small mat in any direction without disturbing the pattern pieces. Being able to turn the mat instead of turning the pieces helps ensure accuracy.

Rotary Cutters

It is helpful to have two sizes of Olfa rotary cutters. The large one can be used for cutting strips and the smaller one for cutting individual pieces. Just like sewing machine needles, the blades for rotary cutting must be sharp. When a blade is dull, it skips. Sometimes, if you will take the cutter apart and clean the blade and parts, you can get a little more life out of it. A third cutter is nice. Put your old blade in it to use for cutting plastic and paper.

Scissors

My favorite pair of scissors is Gingher® #5. They have sharp points and are comfortable to hold. Another favorite is a little 4" pair of tatting scissors made by Dovo®. One blade has a very fine point, and the other has a little a rounded nub on the tip. These are perfect for appliqué. You will also need a pair of scissors to use exclusively for paper and template materials.

Rulers

A 6½" x 24" Quilter's Rule™ rotary cutting ruler is my old standby for cutting large strips. It has a grid grip on the back, which I like. For cutting smaller strips, I use a 4" x 8" rotary ruler. My favorite rulers, of course, are the Dear Jane® Tools. A 5" square is perfect for sizing your blocks and cutting small pieces, and a triangle ruler is good for trimming and cutting all those pretty triangles.

Thread

For the past five or six years, there has been a controversy about using silk thread on cotton fabric. Purists say that silk thread is for silk fabric; cotton thread is for cotton fabric. They advise not to mix the two. When I first heard about this, I was thrown for a loop. I loved appliquéing with silk thread on cotton fabric. I was in an absolute quandary over this controversy. I told myself to "get a grip" because, I had bought quite a few silk kimonos in Japan that were more than

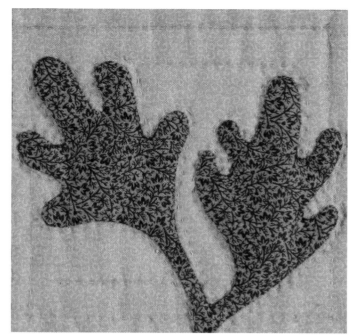

Block F–8, page 61.

100 years old, and the only holes in them were from wear, not from thread breakage. My decision to continue to use silk thread was made when I realized that in 100 years I hope to be singing with the angels and will not be concerned about silk thread versus cotton fabric. Life is so short. If you enjoy using silk thread, I say use it. The pleasure we have in stitching is what matters.

I do recommend that, when you use cotton thread, you use three-ply. That is what I'm using now. A medium gray works well for all types of sewing.

Needles

Clover® has a nice, thin, straight pin. For needles, I use John James #11 and #12 sharps for hand-piecing and appliqué. I also like to use a #11 straw or milliner's needle for the easier appliqué. A straw needle is a bit longer than a sharp, so it bends more readily after a short time of use. If you like using a straw needle, just toss it when it bends. Gone are the days when a woman had only one needle, which she had to use for many years.

Thimbles

There are so many thimbles on the market that it is impossible to critique them all. You can buy a sterling designer thimble, or you can get one from a department store. My friend Rebecca swore by the thimble I bought her on a trip and used it for everything. I paid a dollar for it. I have her thimble, and it is one of my greatest treasures.

Suffice it to say, in my opinion, you must use a thimble to hand-quilt. I have noticed that about half my students use a thimble to hand-piece and appliqué as well. It seems to depend on how you learned to sew. If you are new to quilting, try using a thimble to quilt.

Your thimble should fit snugly on your middle finger so that it doesn't slip as you stitch. It must be strong, with dimples deep enough so you can push four or five stitches onto the needle without the needle's slipping out of a dimple. If you have never worn a thimble before, try wearing it around the house until you forget that it's on your finger. At that point, you will be ready to use it for quilting.

Marking Tools

Berol™ has good marking pencils in silver and gold. I also use Clover's Chalkoliner or tailor's chalk for dark fabrics. A simple #2 pencil is good for marking light to medium fabrics. For marking needle-turn appliqué, I use a .01 Pigma™ pen. Another good marking tool is the Hera marker. It is plastic and makes a crease, rather than a mark, on the fabric.

When I was at the James Museum in Nebraska, I saw an early 1800 appliqué quilt. It was gorgeous with tiny, tiny stitches, but I laughed out loud. The quilting lines were marked with a pencil! There you have it. After 200 years, we quilters are still looking for the perfect marking tool.

Template Materials

Freezer paper – Freezer paper is my number one choice of template material for hand and machine-sewing and appliqué. You can see through it to trace and can use it several times before it begins to wear.

Mylar® – When I make something that has repeating elements, such as leaves, or when I am hand piecing the same block several times, I make templates of Mylar. Available at engineering supply stores, it comes plain or grided and can be used hundreds of times.

Plastic – Template plastic is the good old standby for quilters. Some plastic is now available that can withstand heat so you can iron your fabric on it.

Address labels – When I was in Troy, New York, a student told me she was using address labels for templates. (I wish I could recall her name.) What a surprise! I'm talking about address labels for your ink-jet printer. They are available in 8½" x 11" sheets. Clear is preferable to white. They leave no residue on the fabric and are reusable. A number of people have had great success with them.

Batting

Selecting quilt batting is like choosing candy from a candy shop. There are 100-percent cotton batts, 100-percent polyester batts, and combinations of the two. There are also silk batts and wool batts. Each one has its place. The batt I seem to always use is a blend of 80 percent cotton and 20 percent polyester. There is a cotton batt currently available that can be quilted about 3" to 6" apart, and I hear it is wonderful to quilt with.

Hoops

The most commonly used hoop is 14" in diameter, which works well for most quilting tasks. My favorite is a 9" x 14" wooden one that I have used for years. It accommodates two DEAR HANNAH blocks perfectly. I realize that some people don't use hoops and still obtain wonderful results. However, I believe that most of us need the stability a hoop provides. An 8" round hoop covers a DEAR HANNAH block quite well, and it gives you the freedom of turning your quilt while you stitch.

Sewing Machine

Your sewing machine must be in good working order. While it is not necessary to have the finest machine on the market, it is necessary that your machine makes a good straight stitch and that you change the needle frequently and have the machine serviced regularly. Respect your machine by keeping it oiled and lint-free. Use a straight-stitch throat plate for easier straight stitching.

Remember the Dear Jane–Dear Hannah motto:

Finished is better than perfect!

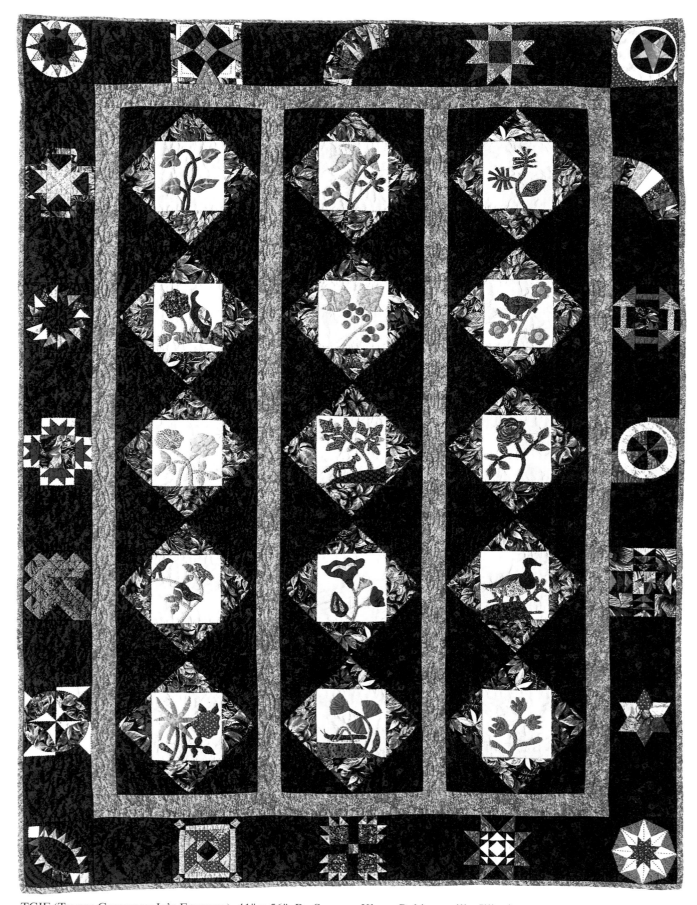

TGIF (THANK GOODNESS IT'S FINISHED), 41" x 56". By Susanne Kleen, Robinsonville, Illinois.

Dear Hannah: In the Style of Jane A. Stickle – Brenda Manges Papadakis

Identifying Blocks

To help you find the blocks you want to make, the rows in MANY HANDS are lettered from A through M. The blocks in each row are numbered 1 through 11 (refer to Block Finder on facing page). The rows in the diagram are color coded to match the "bar" containing the block name and location number with each pattern.

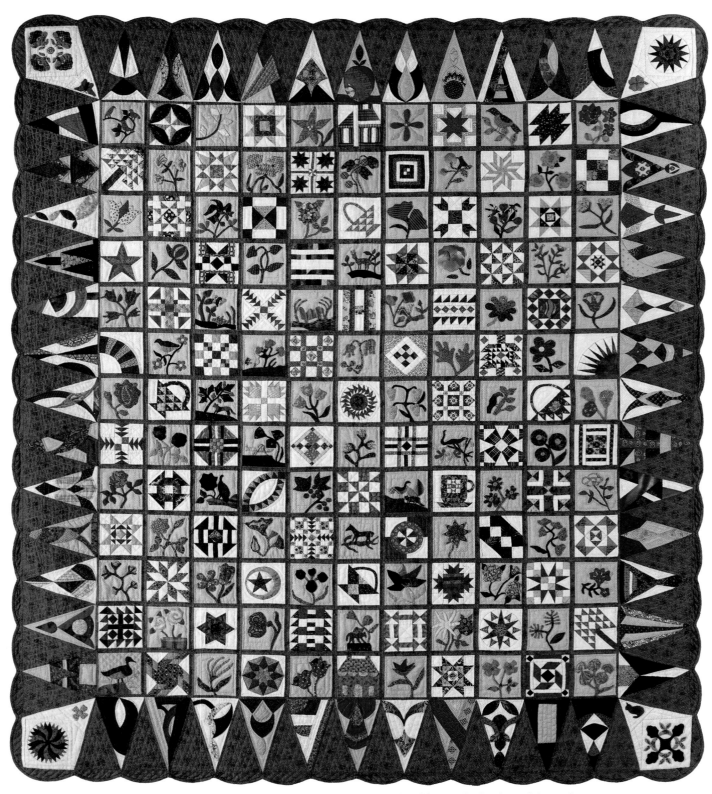

MANY HANDS MAKE LIGHT WORK, 82" X 72". Group quilt, quilted by Amish friends. Collection of the author.

Dear Hannah: In the Style of Jane A. Stickle – Brenda Manges Papadakis

Block Finder

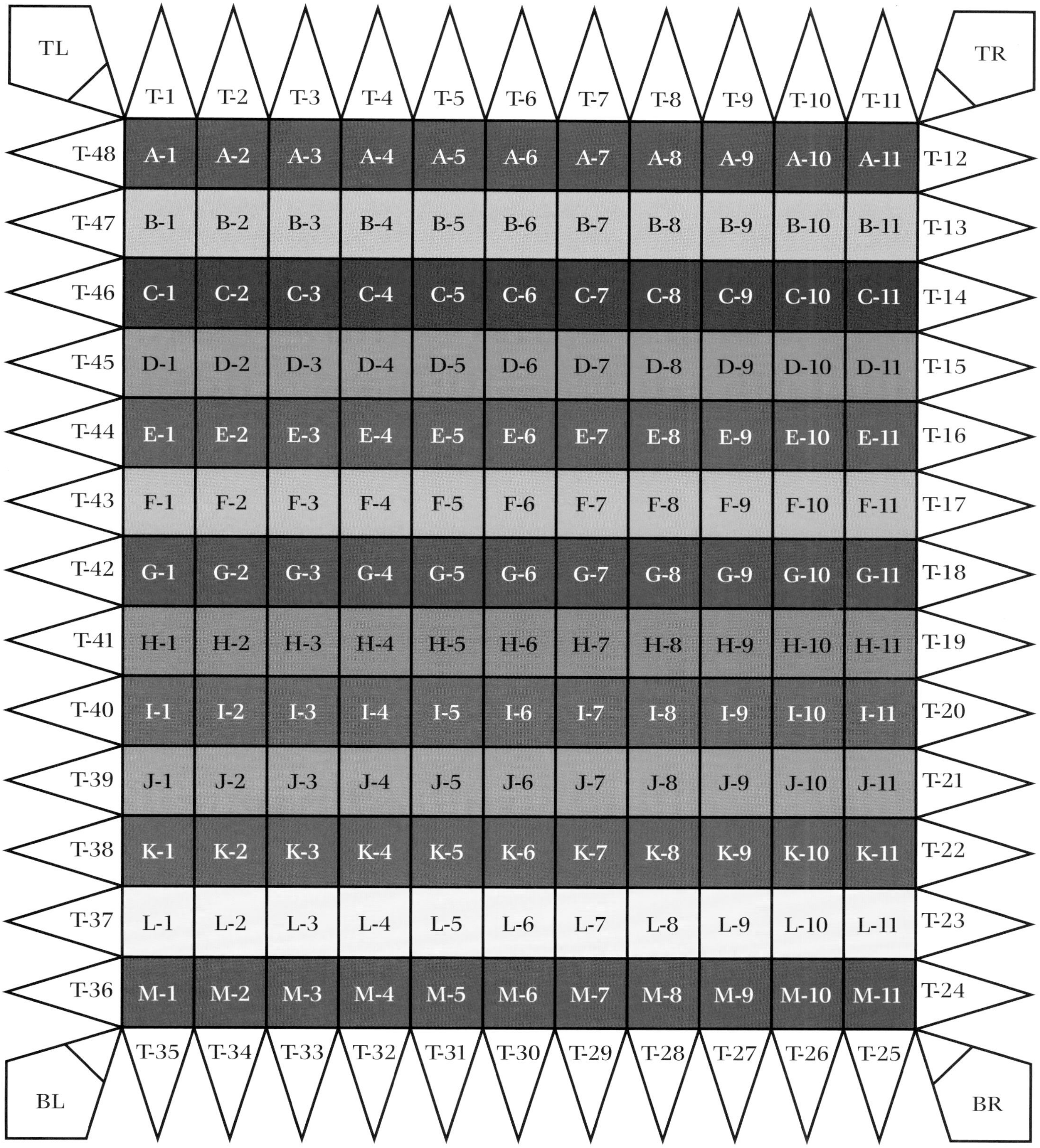

	T-1	T-2	T-3	T-4	T-5	T-6	T-7	T-8	T-9	T-10	T-11	
T-48	A-1	A-2	A-3	A-4	A-5	A-6	A-7	A-8	A-9	A-10	A-11	T-12
T-47	B-1	B-2	B-3	B-4	B-5	B-6	B-7	B-8	B-9	B-10	B-11	T-13
T-46	C-1	C-2	C-3	C-4	C-5	C-6	C-7	C-8	C-9	C-10	C-11	T-14
T-45	D-1	D-2	D-3	D-4	D-5	D-6	D-7	D-8	D-9	D-10	D-11	T-15
T-44	E-1	E-2	E-3	E-4	E-5	E-6	E-7	E-8	E-9	E-10	E-11	T-16
T-43	F-1	F-2	F-3	F-4	F-5	F-6	F-7	F-8	F-9	F-10	F-11	T-17
T-42	G-1	G-2	G-3	G-4	G-5	G-6	G-7	G-8	G-9	G-10	G-11	T-18
T-41	H-1	H-2	H-3	H-4	H-5	H-6	H-7	H-8	H-9	H-10	H-11	T-19
T-40	I-1	I-2	I-3	I-4	I-5	I-6	I-7	I-8	I-9	I-10	I-11	T-20
T-39	J-1	J-2	J-3	J-4	J-5	J-6	J-7	J-8	J-9	J-10	J-11	T-21
T-38	K-1	K-2	K-3	K-4	K-5	K-6	K-7	K-8	K-9	K-10	K-11	T-22
T-37	L-1	L-2	L-3	L-4	L-5	L-6	L-7	L-8	L-9	L-10	L-11	T-23
T-36	M-1	M-2	M-3	M-4	M-5	M-6	M-7	M-8	M-9	M-10	M-11	T-24
	T-35	T-34	T-33	T-32	T-31	T-30	T-29	T-28	T-27	T-26	T-25	

TL   TR

BL   BR

When you were born, you cried and the world
rejoiced. Live your life so that when you die, the
world cries and you rejoice.

—Cherokee proverb

Hallelujah!

What a special, wonderful day! A beautiful granddaughter! You are a precious gift from God, and I feel blessed to hold you in my arms.

I am so flooded with emotion, laughing and crying all at the same time. I look into your precious little face and see the faces of all who have gone before you. Yet you, Hannah, are unique in all the world.

You're only a few hours old, and I want to tell you one hundred stories on this very day. Right now, I'm content just to hold you in my arms, feeling your soft skin, kissing your little fingers and toes.

There sits your mom, all rosy cheeked and full of smiles. All she's ever wanted since she was a young girl is to be a Mommy. She loves you very much and will be a wonderful Mommy.

Children call their grandmothers all kinds of endearing names, Hannah. For your mother, it is "Mamaw" or "Gran." Other children may call their grandmothers "Oma" or "Nana." I'll be your "Yiayia," just as I am for Ben. It is Greek for grandmother. I think it was chosen because it's one of the first words a child can say!

I am sitting in the hospital on your birthday with a quilt to bind for Dear Jane. In fact, the quilt is "Eaton's Crossroads," made in honor of your great-grandmother, Johnnie Mae. What quilt have I made for you? When your Mommy told me you were coming, I went crazy, pulling fabric for a dozen quilts. What a mess I made! Yours is the little pink and brown double nine-patch Baby Jane doll quilt.

God bless you, Hannah, and may your life be healthy and happy.

Welcome, Little One!

yiayia

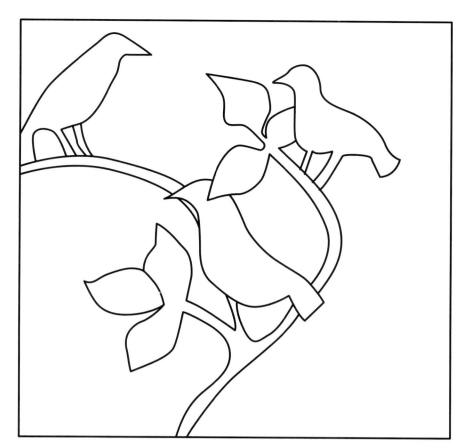

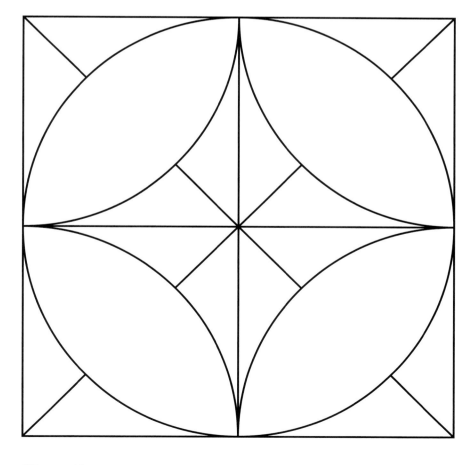

A–3
Dragon Tail

A–4
Paul's Patrol

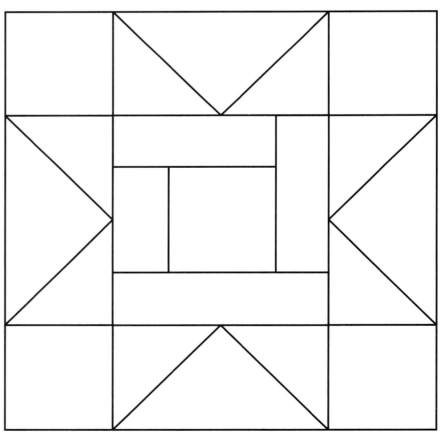

Dear Hannah: In the Style of Jane A. Stickle – Brenda Manges Papadakis

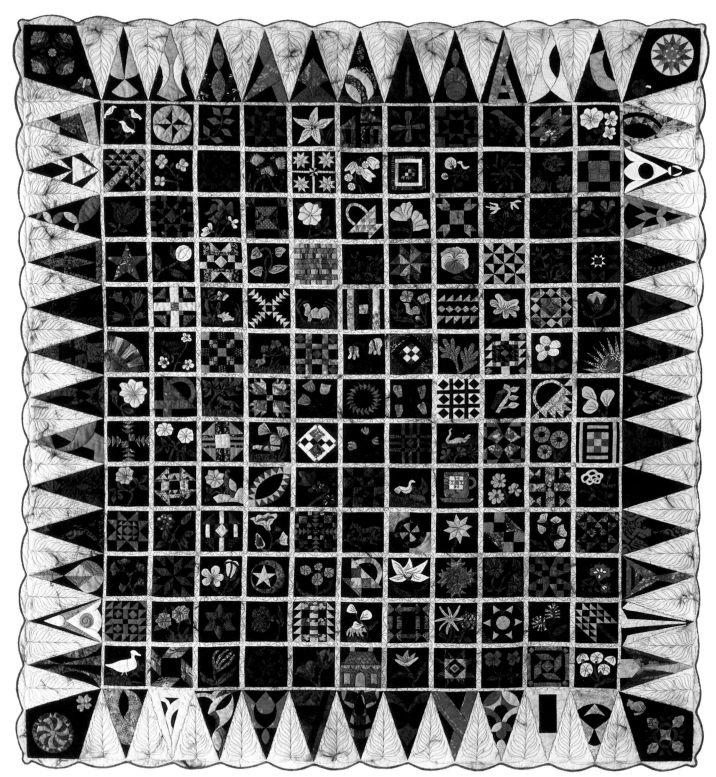

EDITH DARLENE, 71" x 80". Made by Edith Shanholt, Elkhart, Indiana. Quilted by Cathy Franks, Indianapolis, Indiana. Collection of the author.

A-5
California Star

A-6
Texas Schoolhouse

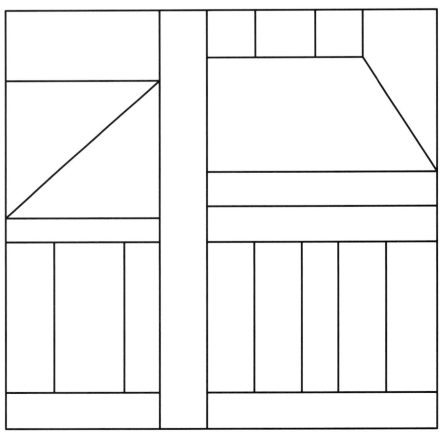

Dear Hannah: In the Style of Jane A. Stickle – Brenda Manges Papadakis

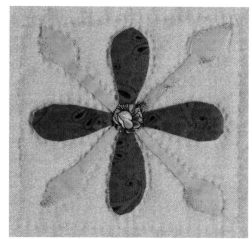

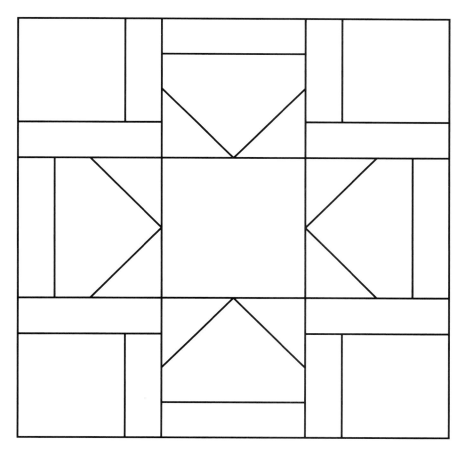

You don't just luck into things as much as you'd like to think you do. You build step by step, whether it's friendships or opportunities.
—First Lady Barbara Bush

Dear Hannah,

This is the best time in my life — blessed with a healthy granddaughter and a new book! *Dear Jane*, was released at Quilt Market today. Now quilters all over the world can know the joy of making their own Baby Jane, and I can play with my Baby Girl.

Jane Stickle also had a reason to play. The day after her forty-eighth birthday, April 9, 1865, General Lee surrendered at the Appomattox Court House. After four long years of brother fighting brother, the Civil War finally ended. Ah, my Little Hannah, the Civil War cannot just be a moment's blur in your history. You must know what a profound effect it had on our country and its families.

The impact of the Civil War on Jane is stated in the corner of her quilt: "In War Time." As an exclamation point she wrote, "5,602 pieces." Jane's world during this time was filled with change and confusion. Counting these little pieces in her quilt gave her a sense of control in her life.

Jane Stickle's amazing quilt of intricate geometric designs was the exception to most quilts made during the Civil War. Most of the quilts made then were simple patterns, like four-patches and nine-patches. You have blocks similar to this time period in your quilt: Town Square (C–4) and From Paducah (J–9).

One of the blessings to come out of this war was that women had an opportunity to be in control of their lives. Whether they lived in the North or South, Little Hannah, women took over the responsibility of their homes, businesses, and farms. They performed these duties well and supplied their troops with food, clothing, and quilts. I'm certain you will have occasions to help your community when you are older.

You're a blessing to me,

yiayia

Dear Hannah: In the Style of Jane A. Stickle – Brenda Manges Papadakis

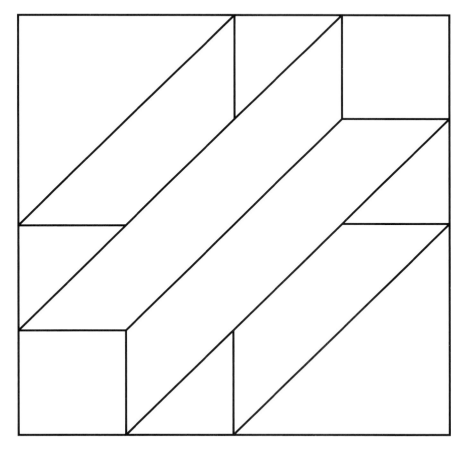

A-11
Ali's Sweet William

B-1
Tennessee Pine

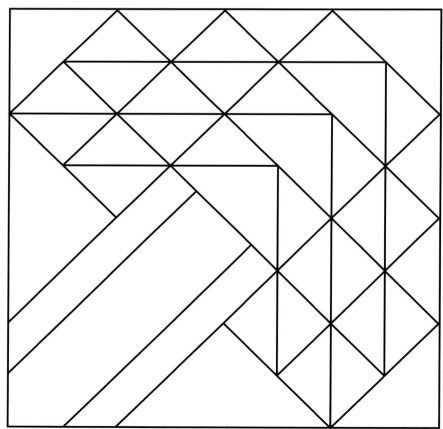

Cautious, careful people, always casting about to preserve their reputation and social standing, never can bring about reform.

—Susan B. Anthony

Precious Hannah,

You're now one year old! It has been a wonderful year. What a joy to be with you as you grow and discover your world. My heart smiles when you plop your little doll face-down on the floor beside you, cover her with your quilt, and pat her on the back. (Joanie says you are destined to be a quilter, because you like to suck the binding of your quilt!)

Yiayia is at the International Quilt Festival. Here are splendid quilts representing quilters all over the world. The best part of the show for me, of course, is Jane Stickle's quilt hanging with an exhibit of Baby Jane quilts made in my first classes.

As I walk around the quilt show, looking at the variety of quilts on display, I keep thinking, "What would Jane Stickle say if she could see all of these bright, contemporary art quilts?" It's only been about twenty years since the art quilt appeared on the horizon of the quilt world, Little One. Quilters like Terrie Hancock Mangat, Nancy Crow, and Yvonne Porcella were pioneers of contemporary quilts. It wasn't easy for them to be accepted in a world of traditional quilts. I wonder what kind of quilts you will make, Hannah…

Next, I walk back to Jane's quilt, thinking about Jane, her life, and the women's movement. "You've come a long way, Baby." It certainly wasn't an easy road for Susan B. Anthony, Elizabeth Cady Stanton, and the other women as they struggled for equal rights. The first Women's Conference was held in Seneca Falls, New York, in 1848. The National Women's History Museum is there. We will go to Seneca Falls, Hannah, so that you may learn about the women who precede you. You will be better equipped to handle the women's issues of your time.

You're my little woman,

yiayia

B-2
Three Sisters

B-3
Omaha Album

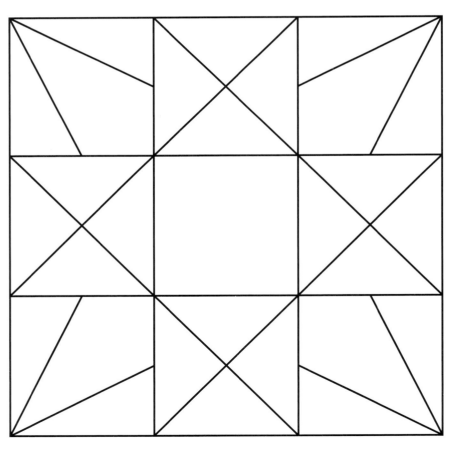

Dear Hannah: In the Style of Jane A. Stickle – Brenda Manges Papadakis

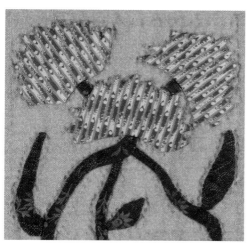

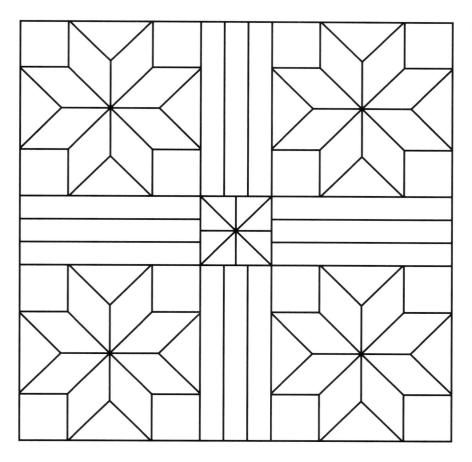

BILLY CREEK, IN
PM
08 JUN
1997

Ladies, we must remind ourselves that the weapon of the vote will be for us, just as it is for any man, the only means of obtaining the reforms we desire. As long as we remain excluded from civic life, men will attend to their own interests rather than to ours.

—Hubertine Auclert

Beloved Little Girl,

Today I attended my first Civil War reenactment. As soon as I heard the booms of cannons, I imagined the soldiers fighting, and burst into tears for the lives lost in this war.

Hannah, the Union Star block (D–1) in your quilt is symbolic of the Civil War. Early in its history, America was in a war for independence from England. The Revolutionary War began in 1775. The plight of women from this war to the Civil War remained basically unchanged.

A woman was not given many educational, economic, or legal rights, not in 1775 nor in 1865. She could not own property or keep her own wages. In cases of divorce, she might not even have custody of her children. Young girls were taught to sew, cook, weave, and mend. If they were lucky, they learned to read and write at home. Hannah, I cannot imagine your not going to school.

One lady of that period was Abigail Smith Adams, wife of the second president of the United States, John Adams. She was a champion of women's rights, believing that boys and girls should be equally educated. When John Adams was preparing to write the Declaration of Independence, she wrote a letter urging him to "Remember the ladies, and be more generous to them than your ancestors…. [We] will not hold ourselves bound to obey the laws in which we have no voice or representation." Neither John Adams nor the writers of the Declaration of Independence paid any heed to Abigail's words. The lives of women and their opportunities were greatly affected by this error throughout the nineteenth century.

Ah, Hannah, it is no surprise that many women in our history organized themselves and worked to obtain basic human rights. We owe them much respect and appreciation for paving the way for us today. I'm certain you will show them this respect by combating unfairness in social situations during your lifetime.

You are wonderful,

yiayia

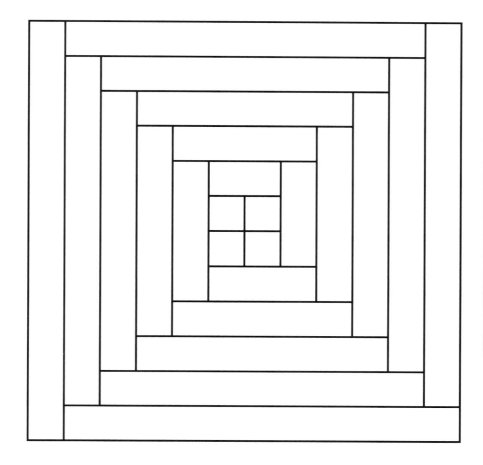

B-8
Partridge in a Pear Tree

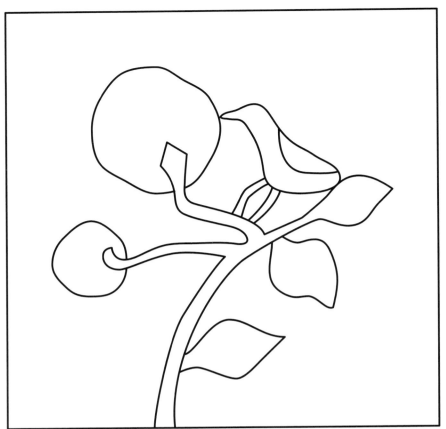

B-9
Tennessee Star

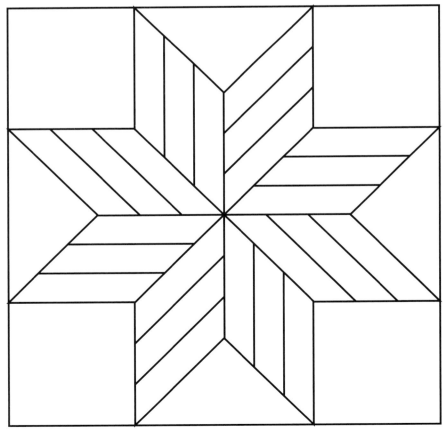

Dear Hannah: In the Style of Jane A. Stickle – Brenda Manges Papadakis

Dear Hannah: In the Style of Jane A. Stickle – Brenda Manges Papadakis

Women's history is the primary tool for women's emancipation.
—Gerda Lerner

Beloved Little Girl,

Here I am in Gettysburg again. I love to come here and meet new quilters. I also like to drive through the battlefields and walk along Baltimore Street. The Civil War battlefields fill one with a sense of history.

Although the Civil War was over in 1865, Yiayia wonders if, in fact, the conflict will ever end. During the first few years after the war, many events unfolded, including the division of women over abolition without women's rights. The women's rights movement was still in progress when Amendment XV was proposed in 1869. This amendment provided suffrage for black men but not women. The amendment passed February 3, 1870, creating another split in the women's movement that was not resolved until 1890. Sweetheart, women were not able to vote for another fifty years.

While progress for women's rights moved too slowly in this country, many wonderful events did occur in the 1870s that made everyone's life easier and more pleasant. Scottish-born Alexander Graham Bell gave us the telephone in 1876. Hannah, I'm certainly glad. How else could I talk with you almost every day? You're so cute, too, because you dance and sing for me, believing I can see your every movement. The year after the telephone, Thomas Edison invented the phonograph. In 1879, he gave us our first light bulb. Now we can really enjoy our music and read our books! What gifts!

It was in 1870 that Salinda W. Rupp made her wonderfully geometric quilt in Pennsylvania. Like Jane's quilt, most of the blocks are Salinda's originals. There are thirty-six of them in your quilt, Hannah. Look at Christopher's Laughter (D–5), with that one little half-square triangle. Salinda's quilt also includes several unusual centers in a traditional Variable Star block. One of those is Olivia's Grace (J–1). There are three more in your quilt. Can you find them?

You are my gift!

yiayia

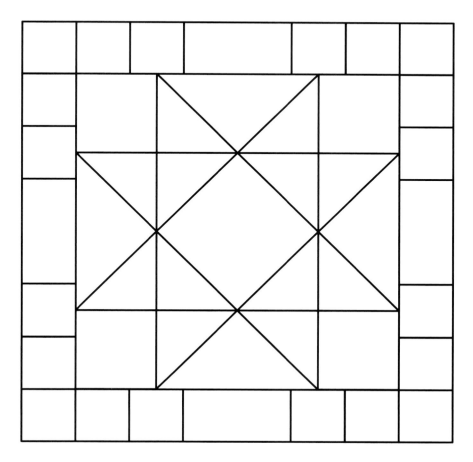

Dear Hannah: In the Style of Jane A. Stickle – Brenda Manges Papadakis

C–3
Mabel's Eagle

C–4
Town Square

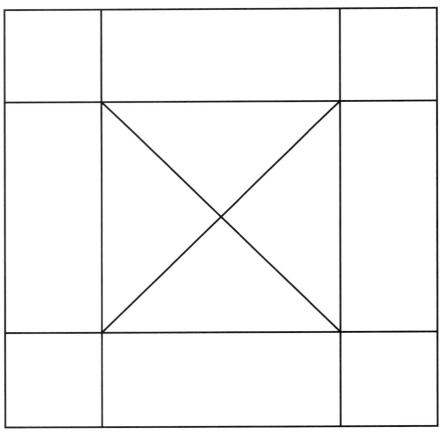

DISTANT STAR, 45" x 45". Made by Lu Ann Krug and quilted by Cathy Franks, both of Indianapolis, Indiana.

C–5
Gillian's Geranium

C–6
Christina's Bounty

Dear Hannah: In the Style of Jane A. Stickle – Brenda Manges Papadakis

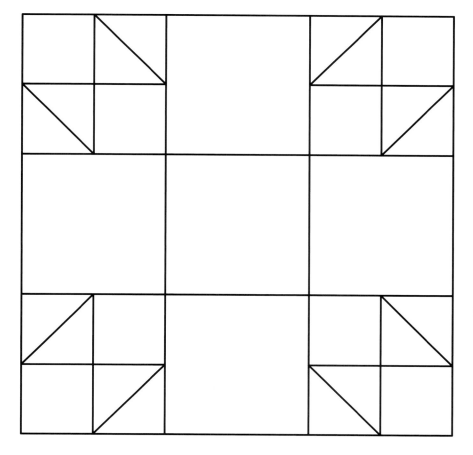

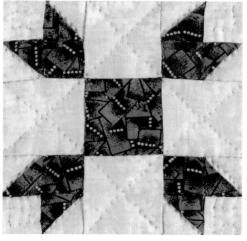

Dear Hannah: In the Style of Jane A. Stickle – Brenda Manges Papadakis

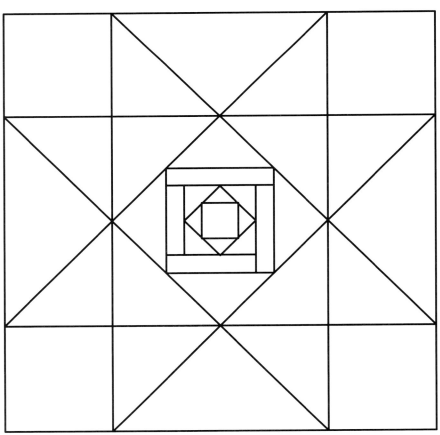

Dear Hannah: In the Style of Jane A. Stickle – Brenda Manges Papadakis

THROUGH THICK AND THIN, 48" x 48". By Connie Clark, Sheridan, Indiana.

C–11
Azalea Friends

D–1
Union Star

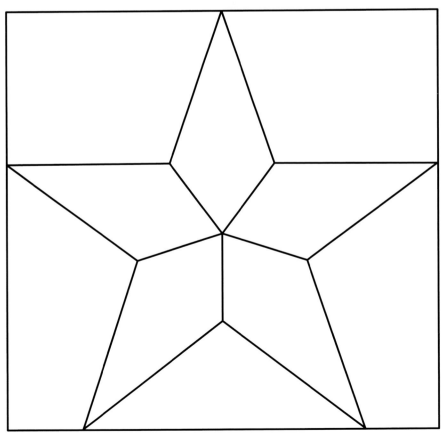

Dear Hannah: In the Style of Jane A. Stickle – Brenda Manges Papadakis

D-2
Love Apple

D-3
Marsha's Maze

I have learned from experience that the greater
part of our happiness or misery depends on
our dispositions and not on our circumstances.
—Martha Washington

Dear Baby Girl,
    Yiayia is growing as you grow. You're barely two years old, and Yiayia is giving you all these history lessons. Sweet-heart, life is just like school. We learn something new every day: meeting people, reading, listening, and watching. In my travels sharing the Jane Stickle quilt, I am meeting so many wonderful people. Each one makes an impression on my heart. In the beginning, I was nervous and shy when I went to give a lecture about Jane Stickle. I gained confidence through the friendships made by sharing Jane's quilt and our lives. Thanks to the Internet, we have friends all over the world. The block in the very center of your quilt, Circle of Friends (G-6), represents these friendships.
    As I teach Jane's quilt, I also meet some women who lack confidence in their abilities. I want to empower them with strength and assurance to use in both quilting and their per-sonal lives. I do this by teaching about women from the past, the forerunners of historic accomplishments through personal toil and tears. I believe this knowledge will give them more power in their own lives. I want to give this same power to you, Precious Child.
    These forerunners are the people who have given us the music you love so well. They are artists, poets, and writers. They are also teachers, scientists, doctors, and soldiers. To know about them is to appreciate life, to love people and the friendships that they provide. This knowledge lets you walk in this world with pride and without fear. Little One, you are growing up at a wonderful time. Many doors are open to you that were once forbidden to women. Acknowledge the historic struggle by working for the women's issues of your time.

You are my teacher,

yiayia

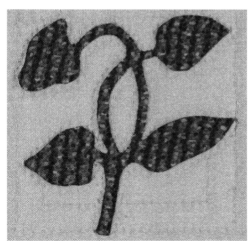

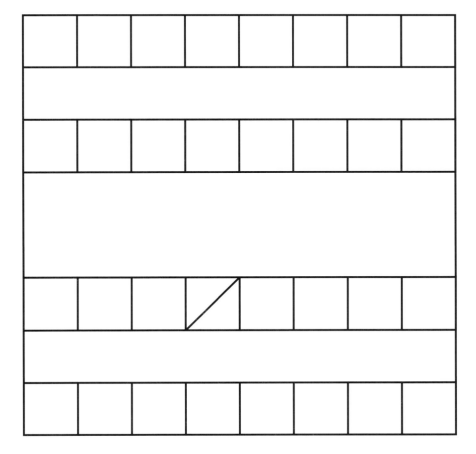

D–6
Cade's Cove

D–7
Sara John's Puzzle

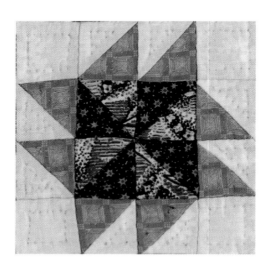

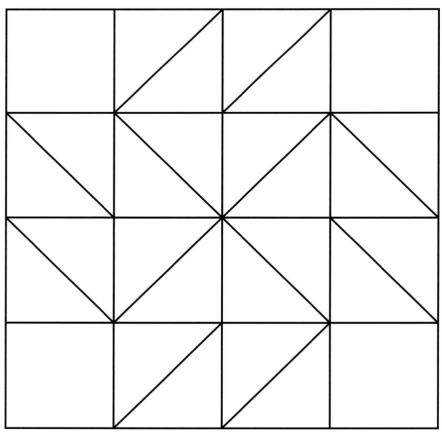

Dear Hannah: In the Style of Jane A. Stickle – Brenda Manges Papadakis

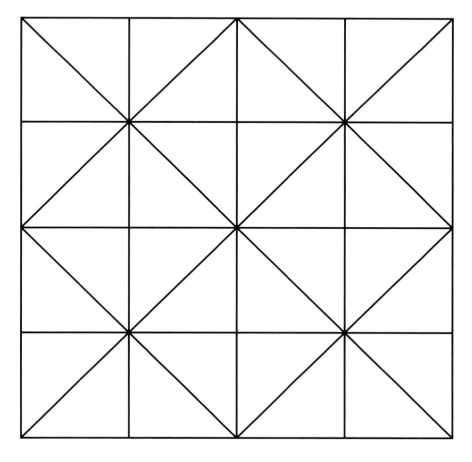

D–10
Birds Of A Feather

D–11
Aubrey's Star

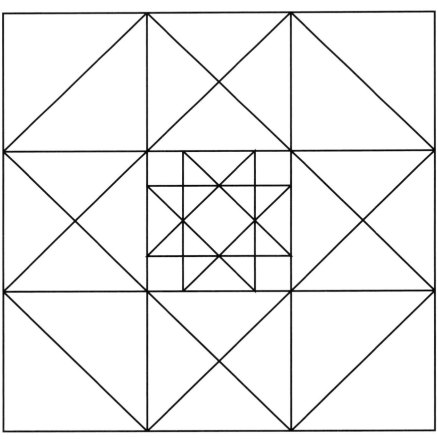

Dear Hannah: In the Style of Jane A. Stickle – Brenda Manges Papadakis

Patchwork? Ah, no! It was memory, imagination, history, biography, joy, sorrow, philosophy, religion, romance, realism, life, love and death; and over all, like a halo, the love of the artist for his work and the soul's longing for earthly immortality.
—Aunt Jane of Kentucky

Ah, Sweet Child,

What a memory you have made for me, sitting on the floor with your basket of "favric," cutting tiny pieces and laying them out in random designs. If we sew them together, you'll have a crazy quilt!

Crazy quilts are made from randomly cut pieces of fancy fabrics, silks, brocades, and velvets that have elaborate embroidered stitches covering the seams of the fabric pieces. These quilts were all the rage during the late nineteenth century.

Oh, Hannah, crazy quilts weren't the only quilts made in the nineteenth century. Women all over the country made beautiful, wondrous quilts. There were elaborate appliqué quilts, which are symbolized in your quilt in the lower-right corner.

There were basket blocks, like Yiayia's Quilting Basket (G–2), and one of Yiayia's favorites, Bear's Paw (G–4), and many hexagon and diamond designs. An example of a hexagon in your quilt is Texas Star (L–3). What fun we'll have, sharing this quilt!

The women's movement made little progress in the East during the last quarter of the nineteenth century. In the West, it was a very different matter. Wyoming granted women the right to vote in 1869 when it was still a territory. Why, Hannah, Susan B. Anthony even encouraged all women to move there!

Wyoming applied for statehood in 1890, and Congress debated approving the application. Members of Congress didn't like the fact that Wyoming allowed women to vote. The Wyoming legislature sent this message to congress, "We will remain out of the Union a hundred years rather than come in without the women." On July 10, 1890, President Benjamin Harrison signed the bill to make Wyoming a state. Utah, Colorado, and Idaho also joined the Union in the 1890s with women's suffrage.

You have my vote!

yiayia

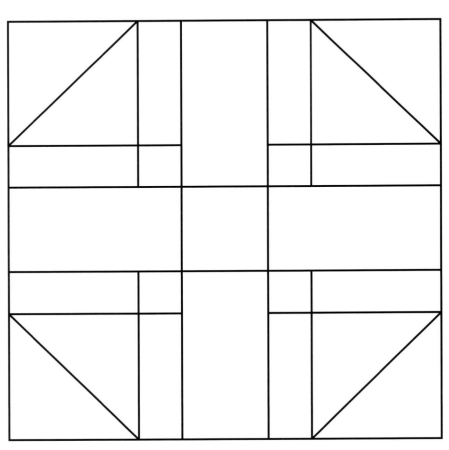

Dear Hannah: In the Style of Jane A. Stickle – Brenda Manges Papadakis

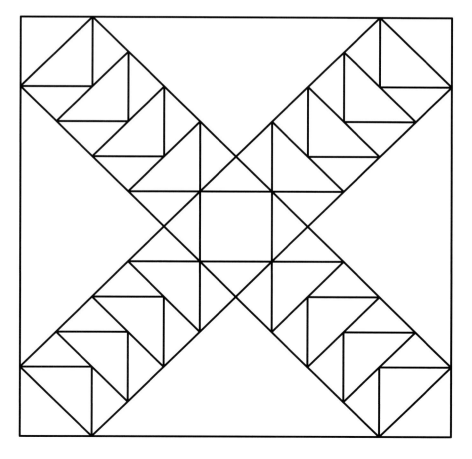

...but now I know that we could never learn to be brave and patient, if there were only joy in the world.

—*Helen Keller*

Dear Little Hannah,

The twentieth century was greeted with excitement and anticipation — much like your family welcomed you! The world had the telephone, the phonograph, electricity, and the horseless carriage. Henry Ford gave us mass-produced cars, and the Wright Brothers flew their first airplane for all of twelve seconds. The "Wizard of Oz" and "Peter Pan" were written, the first Teddy Bear was made, and Beatrix Potter gave us "Peter Rabbit."

In a single day, more than 10,000 people passed through Ellis Island to the Land of Opportunity. People were hopeful for continued industrial progress and prayed for world peace. Where were the women at the turn of the century? One of them, Madame Marie Curie, was the first female to receive a Nobel Prize. She shared the physics prize in 1903 with her husband, Pierre, and another French physicist. In 1911, Madame Curie won the Nobel Prize again, this time in chemistry, for her work on radioactive elements. Hannah, do you think you might want to dedicate your life to a career in science?

Another female making her mark at the turn of the century was Helen Keller, a student at Radcliff College. She was deaf and blind from a childhood illness, yet she graduated cum laude in 1904, with the help of her companion and teacher Anne Sullivan. Not only did she work for the blind, she also worked for women's rights and racial equality. Helen Keller is an example of determination for all of us. Helen's Rose (I–1) in your quilt is named for this remarkable lady.

And what's my little Hannah doing today? You're fascinated with language and imitate everyone. You sing, "Yankee Doodle," "Jesus Loves Me," and "You are my Sunshine" at the top of your voice. You also laugh at Yiayia's silly old songs.

Need I mention that you are also very stubborn? Papou really laughs when you and I are in a standoff. He always says, "What are you going to do now Yiayia? You have one as stubborn as yourself!"

You're so precious, willful one,

yiayia

Dear Hannah: In the Style of Jane A. Stickle – Brenda Manges Papadakis

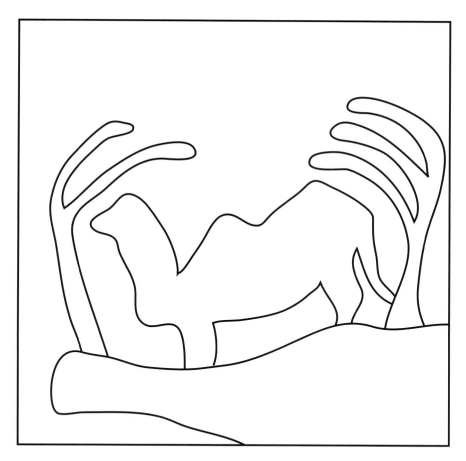

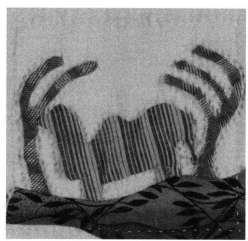

E–7
Gillian's Peacock

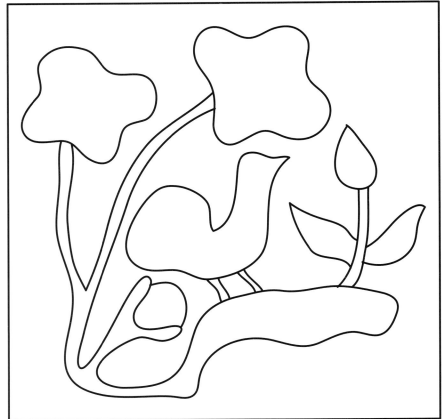

E–8
Road to Calamata

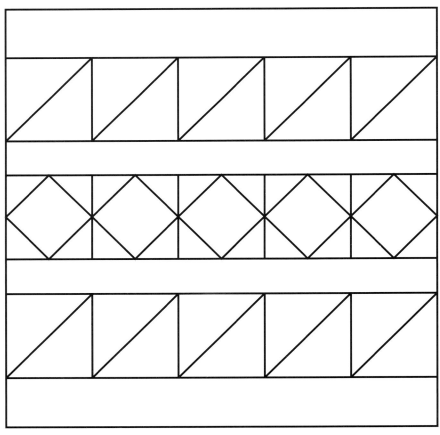

Dear Hannah: In the Style of Jane A. Stickle – Brenda Manges Papadakis

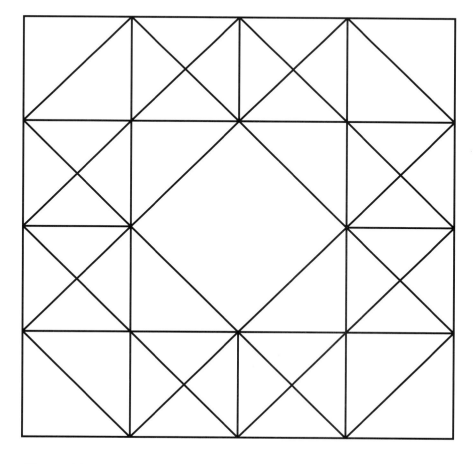

A WALK IN THE GARDEN, 33½" x 33½". By Kathleen Moak, Hixson, Tennessee.

Dear Hannah: In the Style of Jane A. Stickle – Brenda Manges Papadakis

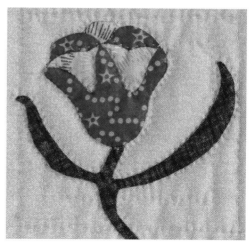

E-11
Shipshewana Tulip

F-1
Gran's Garden

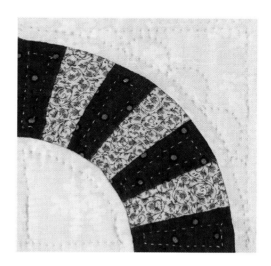

F–2
Morning Call

F–3
John's Checkers

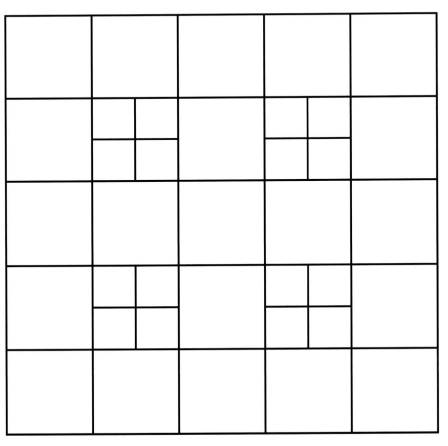

Dear Hannah: In the Style of Jane A. Stickle – Brenda Manges Papadakis

SAN ANTONIO, TX 78201
PM
22 AUG
1998

Parliaments have stopped laughing at women suffrage, and politicians have begun to dodge! It is the inevitable premonition of coming victory.
—*Carrie Chapman Catt*

Dearest Hannah,

What a special day! Uncle Jason and Aracely were married! Immediately, we have a whole new branch to add to the family tree. We are blessed this day, Little One. Aracely was a beautiful bride. You were adorable with your little basket of flower petals. You thought the mariachi band was there just for you, and you danced all over the floor.

Ah, Hannah Lou, let's go back to another August celebration, August 26, 1920. Glorious Day! Congress finally passed Amendment XIX giving women the right to vote. Talk about dancing! The twentieth century took a new direction on this day. Guess what state was the last to vote for the Amendment? Our own Tennessee. There is a block in your quilt that celebrates this very occasion, Tennessee Star (B–9).

Of course, I have to tell you the story, Little Girl. Thirty-five states had voted for the amendment and eight had vetoed it. For ratification, we needed thirty-six votes. Tennessee seemed the last hope for women to be able to vote.

Harry Burn was a twenty-four-year-old Tennessee legislator. He carried a note in his pocket from his mother telling him to vote for the amendment, so he voted "aye." His vote broke the tie.

Harry Burn's mother, Febb Ensminger, couldn't vote. As a widow in Mouse Creek, she managed the family farm after her husband died. As a single parent, she also kept her children in school until they all finished college. Ms. Ensminger had told her son it was wrong that the hired hands on her farm could elect those who governed her life, and she had no say in the matter. After the vote was taken, Burns said, "I knew that a mother's advice is always safest for her boy to follow, and that my mother wanted me to vote for ratification." Ah, Hannah, if only all little boys followed their mother's advice.

You get my vote!

yiayia

F–4
Little Red Rooster

F–5
Hopscotch

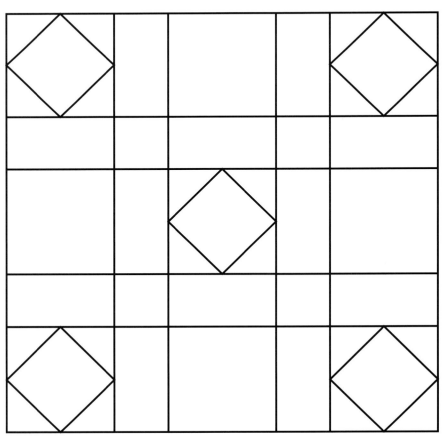

Dear Hannah: In the Style of Jane A. Stickle – Brenda Manges Papadakis

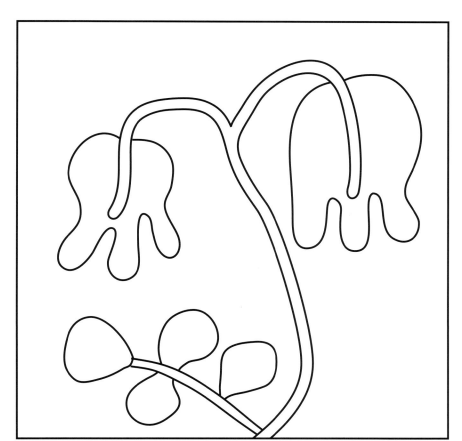

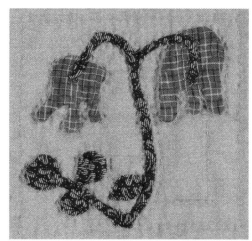

F–7
Tic Tac Toe Plus

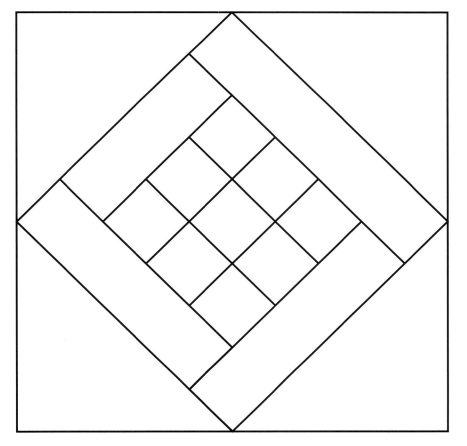

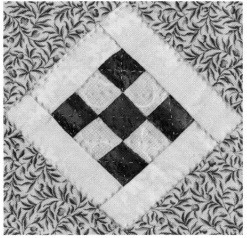

Thanks Again, 67" x 67½" By Kathleen Schaffer Saunders.

Dear Hannah: In the Style of Jane A. Stickle – Brenda Manges Papadakis

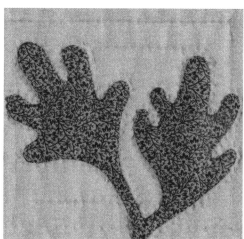

F–9
Which Way to Oz?

F–10
My Flower

F–11
Lady Liberty

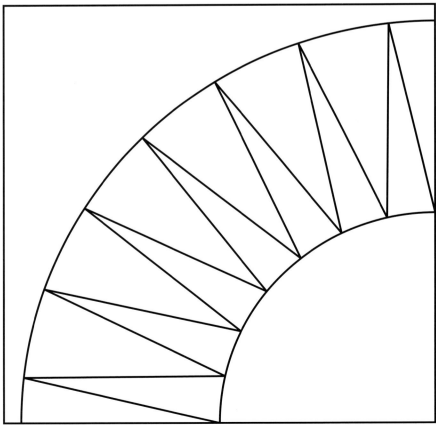

Dear Hannah: In the Style of Jane A. Stickle – Brenda Manges Papadakis

If we would build on a sure foundation in friendship, we must love friends for their sake rather than for our own.
—Charlotte Brontë

Sweet Hannah,

As I drove to Goshen today, I thought of all the kind and generous people I meet as I travel and teach about Jane Stickle and her quilt. This country is filled with wonderful people, Hannah. Some of the most precious people are those here in the Shipshewana area. Well, yes, I'm a little biased – the Maple Leaf Quilt Guild there adopted me!

Shipshewana is an Amish community in Indiana, and "Amish" means "quilt" to Yiayia. The Amish were not always quilters. They learned to quilt from their Pennsylvania Dutch neighbors in the mid–1800s. In fact, the most treasured Amish quilts are those made between 1875 and 1940. Some of these quilts were made of wool dyed by the makers.

Basically, there are three shapes in an Amish quilt: the square, the triangle, and the rectangle. The tops of their quilts have strong, graphic designs made from solid colors, including black and brown. Many of the fabrics, Hannah, are scraps of children's clothing. Amish quilts are pieced on the sewing machine. The quilting, on the other hand, is done by hand and is quite elaborate. I can just imagine you now, Sweetheart, in your own little dress with a bonnet and apron. Rabbit's Paw (C–8) and Churn Dash (I–2) in your quilt are a tribute to our Amish friends. In fact, "Many Hands Make Light Work" was quilted by one of these friends.

The Amish have a simple lifestyle with no electricity or modern conveniences. Both men and women work nearly all day. The men tend the fields and do farm chores. The women take care of the home, cook, and tend to the needs of the family. When the Amish go into town, they ride in a horse–drawn buggy. The Amish community provides a close-knit fellowship both in the church and with the neighbors.

One day, you and I will take a trip to Shipshewana, Hannah. Maybe we can ride in a buggy.

I love you,

yiayia

G–1
Penny's Peony

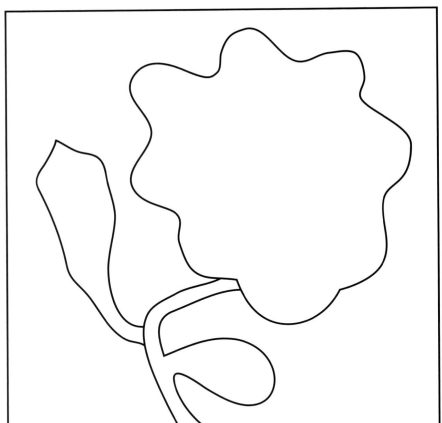

G–2
Yiayia's
Quilting Basket

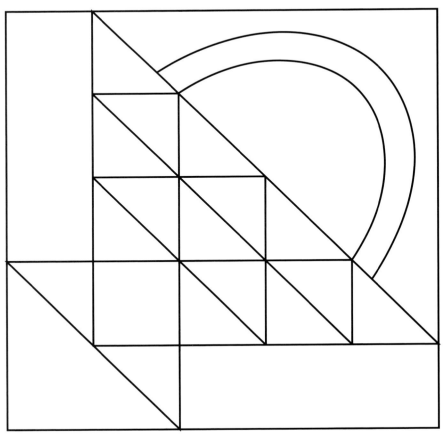

Dear Hannah: In the Style of Jane A. Stickle – Brenda Manges Papadakis

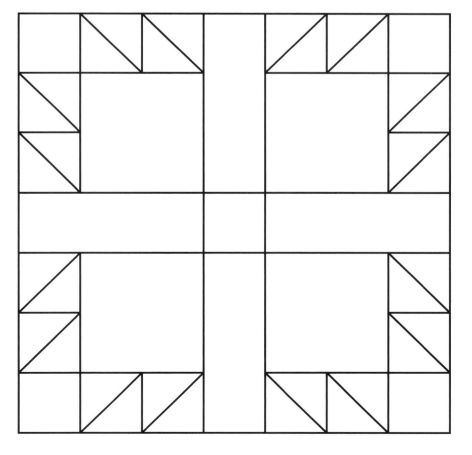

G–5
The Flower Friends

G–6
Circle of Friends

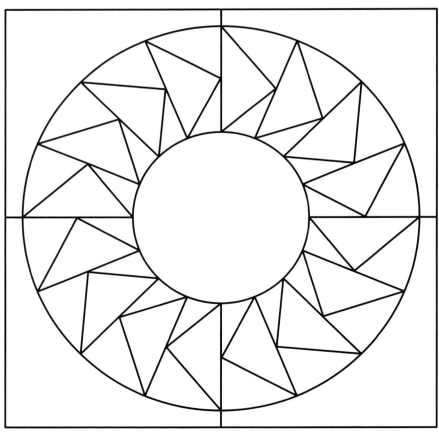

Dear Hannah: In the Style of Jane A. Stickle – Brenda Manges Papadakis

A great gift to one's child is knowledge.
—Christine de Pisan

Dearest Hannah,

Praise God! You have a baby brother, Nathan Alexander. We went to the hospital to meet him, and you held him in your arms. Later, I tried to explain to you that we have an endless supply of love. "You were born and we love you, and now Nathan is here and we love him too." You looked at me for a few seconds and asked, "Did you make him a queeeult?" That's my girl! You do have a block named for Nathan in your queeeult. It is Nathan's Wagon (J-11).

Yesterday, we were in a quilt shop. You came running to me with some fat quarters tied with a ribbon. "Look Yiayia – a present!" They were your favorites, reproductions from the 1930s. Of course, we took them home. Right now, you use fat quarters as little quilts, spreading them all over the floor and then folding them and putting them in your stash. You love to see the tiny kitties, lambs, and children playing in 30s fabrics.

Precious, after women got the vote in 1920, there was a "new woman" in America; she was liberated. As much as you love to "dress up," Hannah, you would really enjoy dressing like a woman of the 1920s. This liberated female cut her hair into a bob, put on powder and rouge, and wore her dresses above her knees. She was even known to go to nightclubs alone and dance the "Charleston!" She was called a "Flapper." Jazz music became the rage, and this period of time is called the "Jazz Age."

Your beloved *Winnie the Pooh* was written in 1926, and Walt Disney made his first movie, *Steamboat Willie*. Penicillin was discovered, and automobiles became affordable for most people. The Roaring Twenties came to an abrupt halt with the stock market crash of 1929. This was a significant event in the century, Hannah, and I know you will revisit it when you are older.

You are both gifts,

yiayia

G-7
Pimientas Calientes

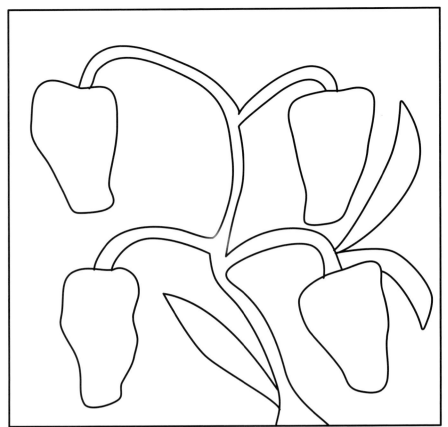

G-8
Cousins Nine

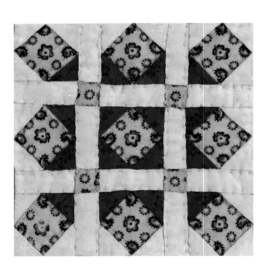

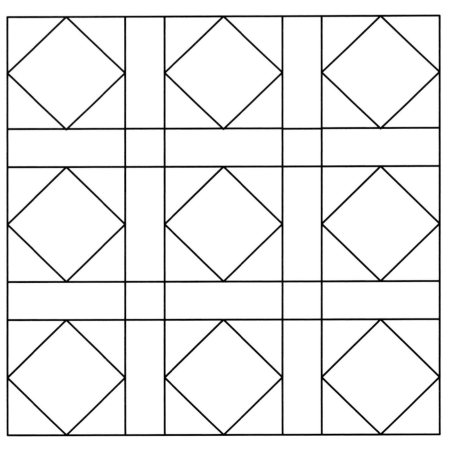

Dear Hannah: In the Style of Jane A. Stickle – Brenda Manges Papadakis

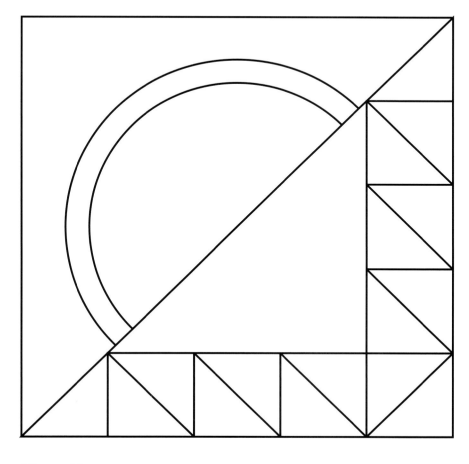

Dear Hannah: In the Style of Jane A. Stickle – Brenda Manges Papadakis

G–11
Three's A Pear

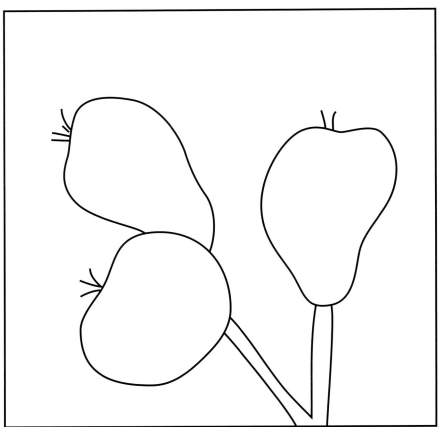

H–1
Meeting of the Minds

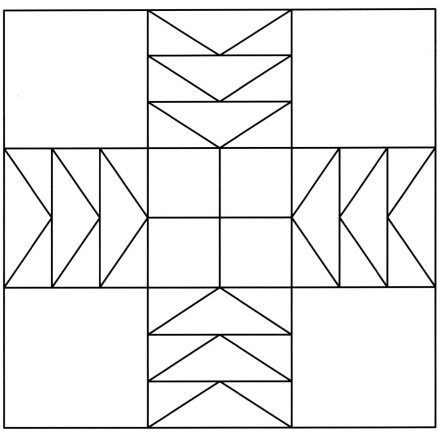

Dear Hannah: In the Style of Jane A. Stickle – Brenda Manges Papadakis

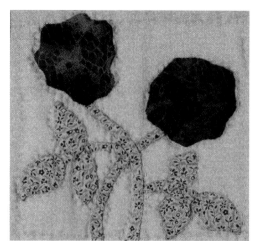

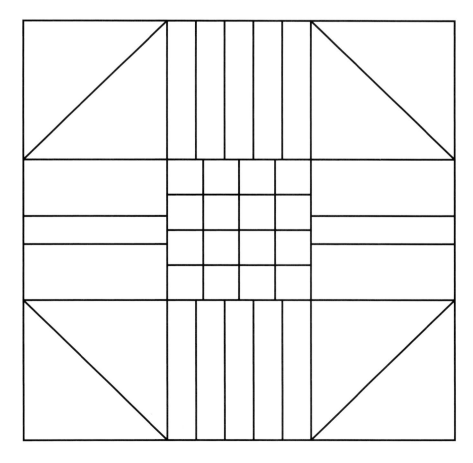

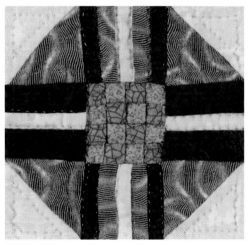

Dear Hannah: In the Style of Jane A. Stickle – Brenda Manges Papadakis

HOT COFFEE, 29½" x 37". By Diane Rode Schneck, New York, New York.

FRIENDS, 26" x 26". By Judy Day, Australia and Vicki Fallobn, Medford, New Jersey. Hand quilted by Virginia Bohnenkamp, Indianapolis, Indiana. Author's collection.

Dear Hannah: In the Style of Jane A. Stickle – Brenda Manges Papadakis

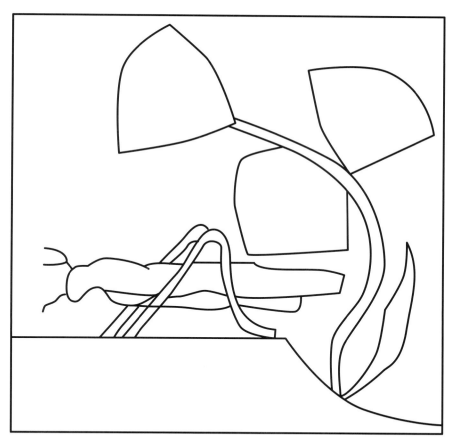

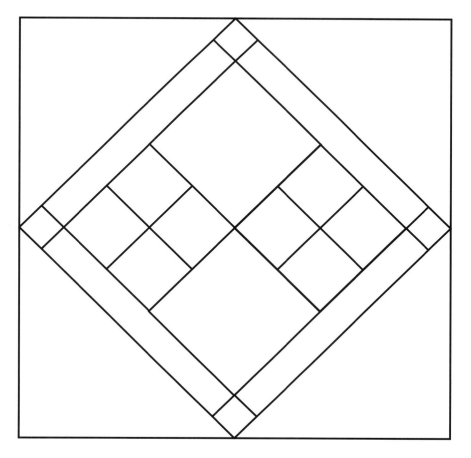

Dear Hannah: In the Style of Jane A. Stickle – Brenda Manges Papadakis

H–6
Sea Creatures

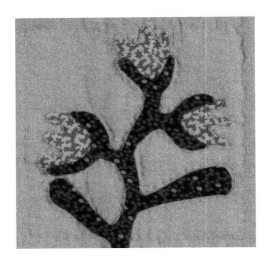

H–7
Keith's Parcheesi

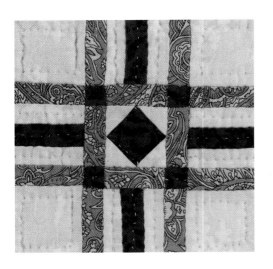

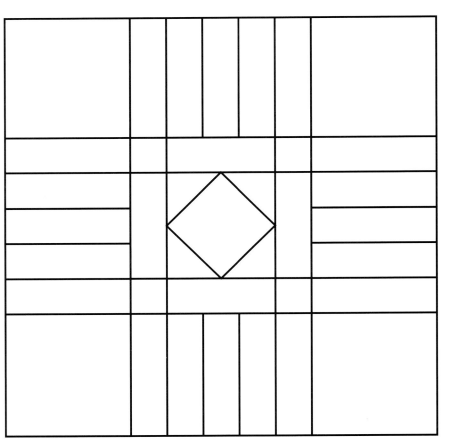

Dear Hannah: In the Style of Jane A. Stickle – Brenda Manges Papadakis

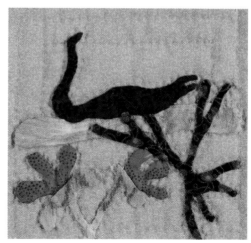

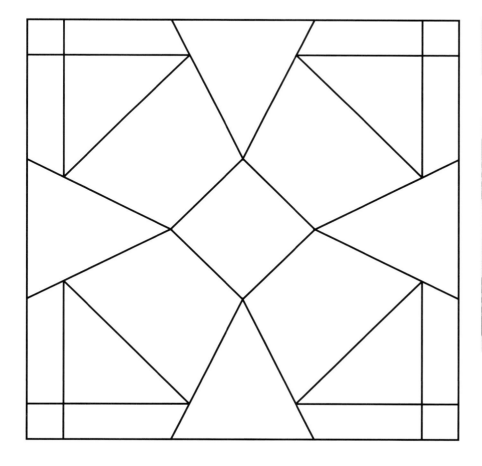

H-10
Posey Posey

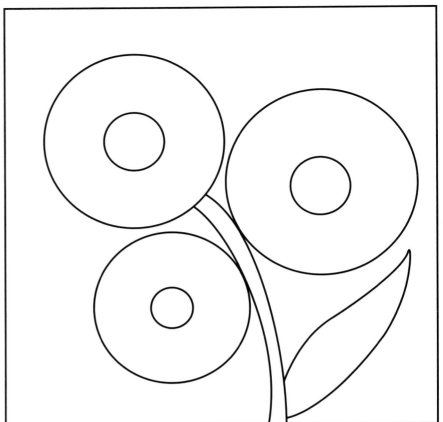

H-11
Nana's Choice

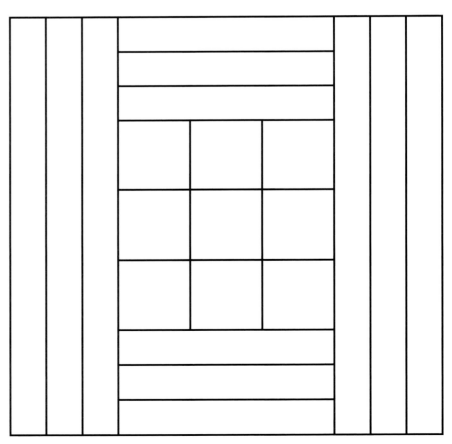

Dear Hannah: In the Style of Jane A. Stickle – Brenda Manges Papadakis

*Nothing in life is to be feared. It is only
to be understood.*

—*Marie Curie*

Precious Hannah,

Here I am in The Quilt Capital of the World! Once more, stunning quilts from all over the world surround me. When I see such beauty, Hannah, I'm overcome with the talents of quilters today.

Just last month when I was sewing blocks for the Dear Jane signature swap, you reminded me of what's really important. I plied you with Molly and Bitty Baby and all their "stuff," and gave you instant access to my fabric stash. You pulled fabric for quilts and patted and talked to your babies. Suddenly you stood up with your hands on your little hips and announced, "Yiayia, we have ever-fang, don't we?" You continued, "We've got our babies, our favric, and our sewing!" Well, Angel, that's just about all of Yiayia's life.

Seeing all the 30s quilts in this show reminded me of the great Sears' National Quilt Contest at the Chicago World's Fair in 1933. This country was in the throes of the Great Depression, but the needlework magazines failed to say anything about the nation's economy. However, the $7,500 prize money enticed 24,000 women to enter their quilts in the contest. While the title of the contest was "Century of Progress," no quilts with this theme won any regional prizes. The judges seemed to prefer "the pretty decorative quilts." What did happen as a result of the Sears' contest was a resurgence of quilting over the next decade. It seemed that almost every home had a quilt in progress.

Many of the same soft pastel quilts they had made in the 20s continued to be made in the 30s. The most popular patterns were Grandmother's Flower Garden, Dresden Plate, Double Wedding Ring, and Sun Bonnet Sue. In fact, Baby Girl, these patterns are still popular today. You have a block in your quilt, Gran's Garden (F–1), that was also popular in the 30s.

You're my little Sunbonnet Sue!

yiayia

I–1
Helen's Rose

I–2
Churn Dash

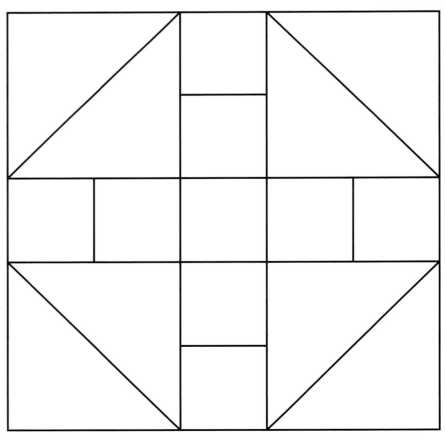

Dear Hannah: In the Style of Jane A. Stickle – Brenda Manges Papadakis

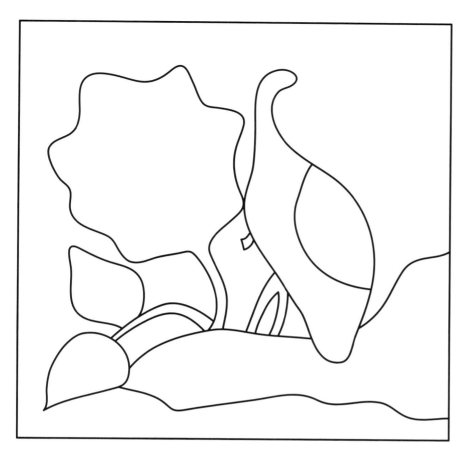

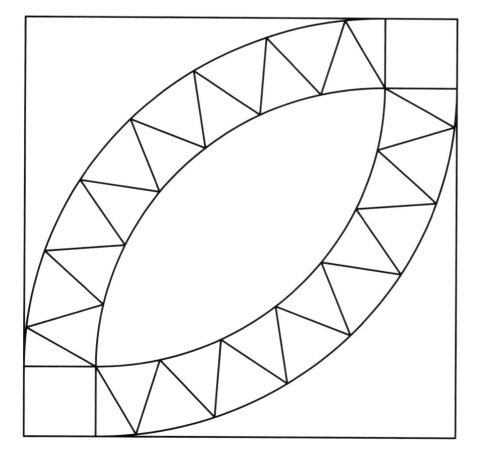

I-4
Pickle Dish

I–5
Texas Wild Wimmin

I–6
Vanishing Point

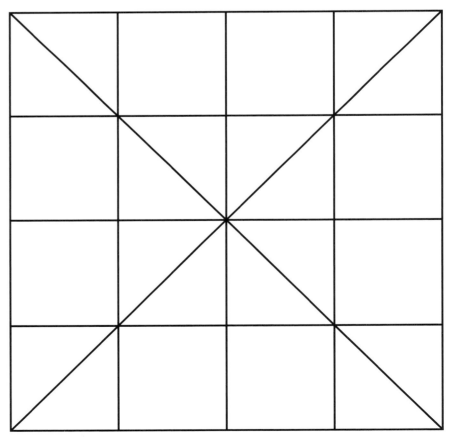

Dear Hannah: In the Style of Jane A. Stickle – Brenda Manges Papadakis

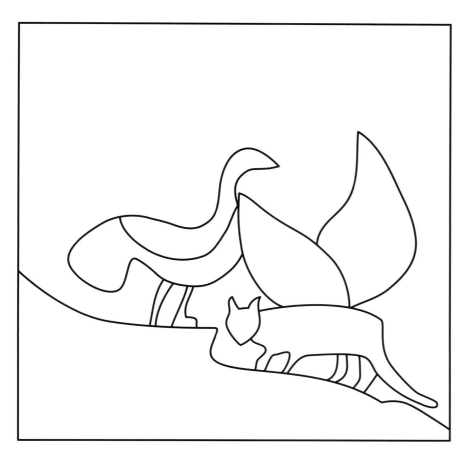

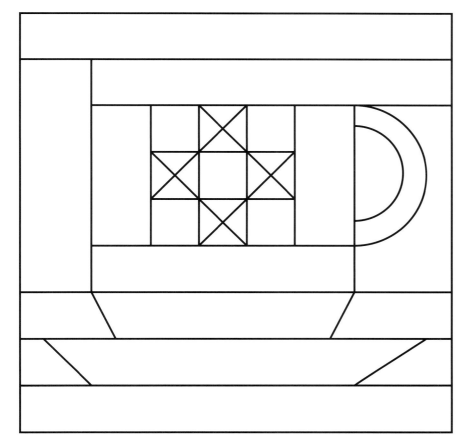

SARA ELEANORA, 71" x 80". Made by Tilde Binger, Denmark. Quilted by Cathy Franks, Indianapolis, Indiana. Collection of the author.

Dear Hannah: In the Style of Jane A. Stickle – Brenda Manges Papadakis

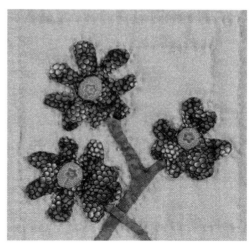

I–11
Solomyn Rose

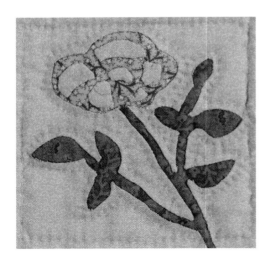

J–1
Olivia's Grace

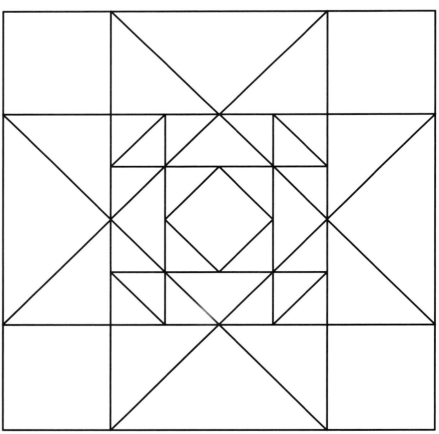

Dear Hannah: In the Style of Jane A. Stickle – Brenda Manges Papadakis

Women must try to do things as men have tried. When they fail their failure must be but a challenge to others.

—*Amelia Earhart*

Beloved Hannah Lou,

The economic depression of the 30s was filled with unemployment, poverty, and homelessness. President Roosevelt offered Americans a New Deal in 1933 that was to stimulate the economy and bring about employment.

At the same time, newspapers were printing quilt patterns, and ladies were collecting them and making quilts. Beautiful appliqué quilts were also being made during this time. (A block in your quilt reminiscent of this appliqué is the Indiana Rose in the upper-left corner kite.) Children's stories and nursery rhyme quilts became popular at this time also. Some of them were colored with crayons and then embroidered.

One of the heroines was pilot Amelia Earhart. In 1928, she flew from Nova Scotia to South Wales, Australia, as the commander in the airplane "Friendship." Two men were the pilots, though she was the one everyone wanted to interview. In 1932, she flew from Newfoundland to Londenberry, Ireland. When she was voted Outstanding Woman of the Year, Ms. Earhart accepted on "behalf of all women." On June 1, 1937, she left Florida for her last flight, a trip around the world with Fred Noonan as her navigator. On July 2, Amelia made her last radio transmission. Despite numerous searches, neither she nor her plane has ever been found. Amelia Earhart's life is a testament to the courage and determination that she wished for every woman. Lady Luck (J-7) is named for this daring woman.

It was also in 1937 that Walt Disney made your favorite movie, "Snow White and the Seven Dwarfs." We've watched Snow White so many times, you have her lines memorized. You lie down with your little hands crossed on your chest, and your eyes squinted closed while you wait for the Prince Yiayia to awaken you with a kiss!

You're my princess,

yiayia

J–2
Max Anna Jane

J–3
Emily Ann's Treasure

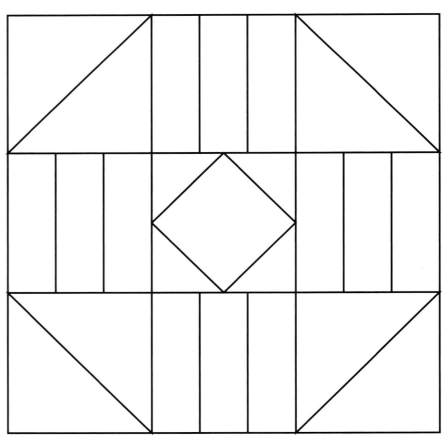

Dear Hannah: In the Style of Jane A. Stickle – Brenda Manges Papadakis

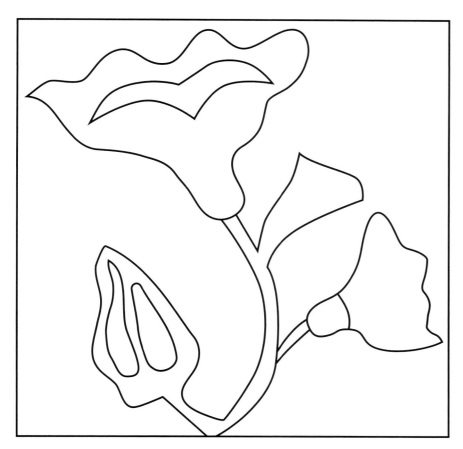

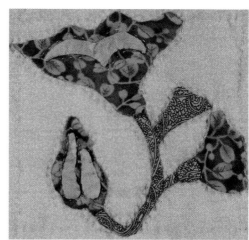

Dear Hannah: In the Style of Jane A. Stickle – Brenda Manges Papadakis

**J-6
Jean Autry**

**J-7
Lady Luck**

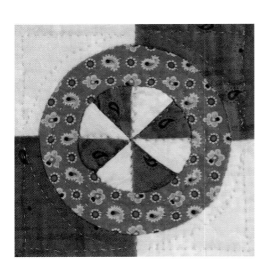

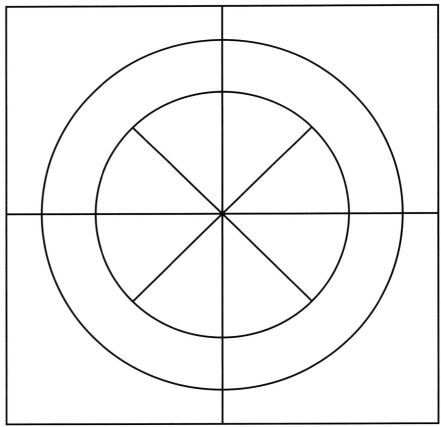

Dear Hannah: In the Style of Jane A. Stickle – Brenda Manges Papadakis

For women there are, undoubtedly, great difficulties in the path, but so much more to overcome. First, no woman should say, "I am but a woman!" But a woman! What more can you ask to be?
—Maria Mitchell

Precious Hannah,

You made your first four-patch on your Tiny Tailor. Your mom and I were so proud we framed it! You're such a cutie sitting at that little sewing machine. You're also becoming quite a "stash hound." In the quilt store, you walked by the 30s fabrics, ran your little hand over the bolts, looked back at me and said, "Yiayia, I'll have this one and this one." Of course, Ma'am. You also proclaimed, "Yiayia, I know you're really my grandmother," as if you had discovered some big secret. The Nana's Choice block (H–11) is named for all of us grandmothers.

Sooner or later, Yiayia has to tell you that the entire world is not fabric, Disney movies, and Barbie dolls. I must tell you a bit about World War I and World War II. These were powerful events in our history that reshaped the world. World War I started in August 1914. According to Papou [Grandpa], this was to be the "war to end all wars." It was fought much like the Civil War: men lined up next to each other and shot. However, the weapons were more sophisticated. World War I ended November 11, 1918, and a peace treaty was signed in Versailles on June 28, 1919. Instead of this being a true peace, it appears to have been but the setting of another war.

Just after the movie Wizard of Oz was released in 1939, Germany invaded Poland, and England declared war on Germany. World War II had begun. However, the United States did not get involved in WWII until two years later. On December 7, 1941, the Japanese bombed Pearl Harbor, and the United States entered the Second World War. The United States was embroiled in WWII for four years, the same amount of time as the Civil War.

It seems to me, Precious, that change results from every war, and much of the change benefits women's equality. In each war since the Revolution, women have stepped forward and contributed to the world of the factory, farm, and business. Each generation became more independent and successful than the previous ones.

I love you,

yiayia

Dear Hannah: In the Style of Jane A. Stickle – Brenda Manges Papadakis

J-8
Passion Flower

J-9
From Paducah

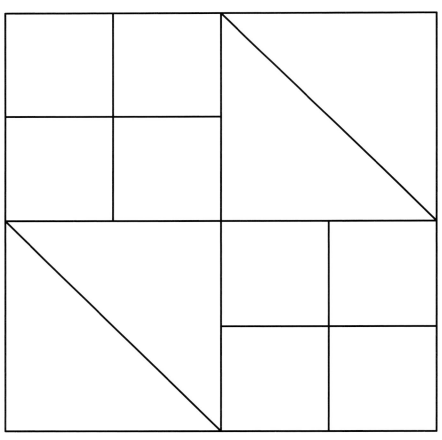

Dear Hannah: In the Style of Jane A. Stickle – Brenda Manges Papadakis

J–10
Bonsai Beauties

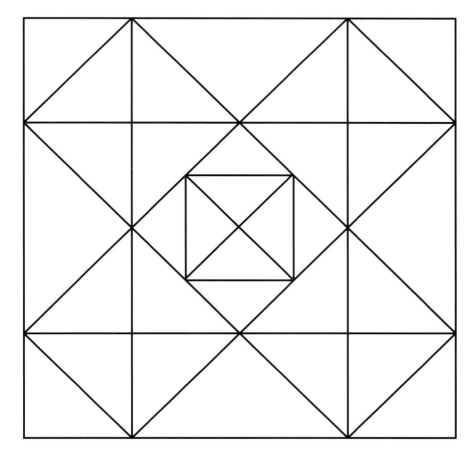

J–11
Nathan's Wagon

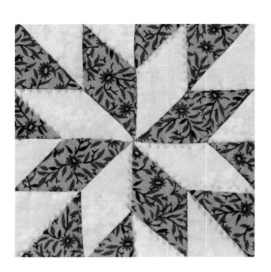

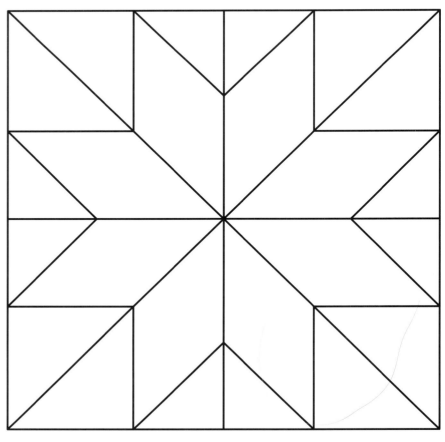

Dear Hannah: In the Style of Jane A. Stickle – Brenda Manges Papadakis

EUROPEAN JANE, 68½" x 75". Group quilt by Dear Jane friends in Europe. Assembled by Claire Baker, Lafayette, Indiana. Quilted by Cathy Franks, Indianapolis, Indiana. Collection of the author.

K-3
Roberta & Mary's Backyard

K-4
Star & Crescent

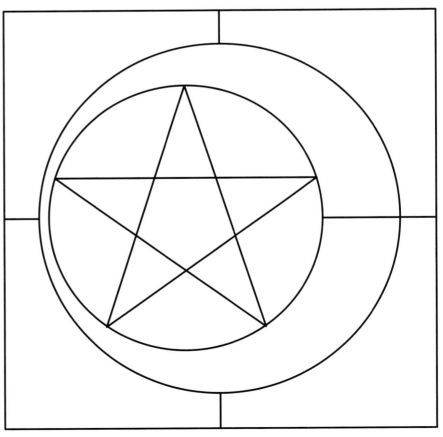

Dear Hannah: In the Style of Jane A. Stickle – Brenda Manges Papadakis

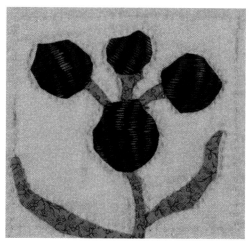

K–5
Walter Joe's
Jack-In-The-Box

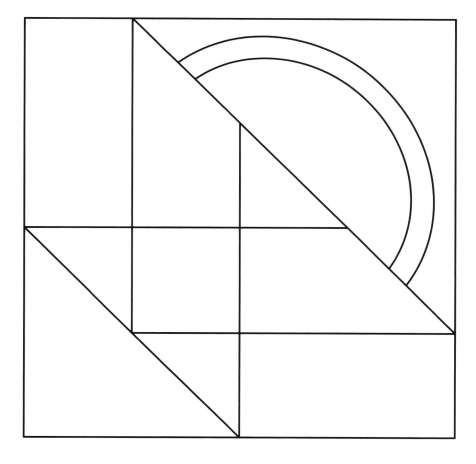

K–6
Joanie's Basket

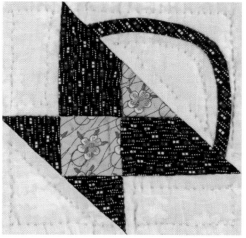

K-7
Sadako

K-8
Ben's Trophy

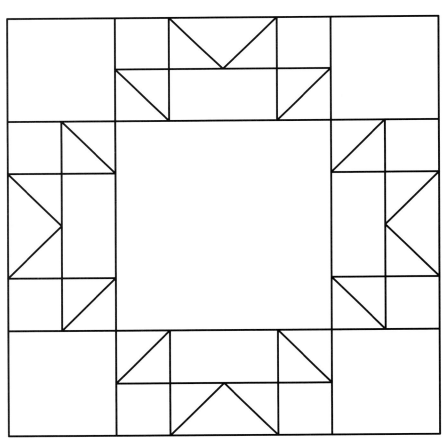

Dear Hannah: In the Style of Jane A. Stickle – Brenda Manges Papadakis

You must tell your children, putting modesty aside, that without us, without women, there would have been no spring in 1945.

—*Rosie the Riveter*

Sweet Hannah,

Happy New Year! We had a wonderful celebration, didn't we? All of the family was there to give hugs and kisses for a New Year and new century. The amazing part was being able to watch the televised productions of other countries' celebrations throughout the evening. I look forward to spending this year with you.

Women dressed as men and fought in all of the wars of the eighteenth and nineteenth centuries. However, it wasn't until World War I that the Armed Forces started using female power. Thirty thousand women served in WWI, most of them nurses – the unsung heroes of every war. Mary's Star block (A–8) is named for our friend Mary, who is a nurse. This block honors the nurses who served in every war.

At home, almost five million women were employed in government offices, public transportation, and industry, including making weapons and building ships. By the time of World War II, 350,000 women were in military uniforms and six million were working in defense plants and offices.

Rosie the Riveter was on a poster that encouraged women to join the work force. Rosie represented all working women. She was strong and showed the power and pride of women in the factories who were welding, building aircraft, and assembling bombs. Women in the Armed Service, as well as in the factories, wore pants publicly for the first time! Women worked outside the home, and they earned good wages. They also filled many responsible positions. It is no wonder that the confidence of women rose to the sky. World War II finally ended in 1945. The United States dropped the first atomic bombs on Nagasaki and Hiroshima. The Japanese surrendered September 12, 1945.

It was during this war that Yiayia was born, and her favorite children's book *The Little Prince* was published. It's a delightful children's book containing a great deal of wisdom for adults. One of my favorite quotes is from the fox, "It is only with the heart that one can see rightly; what is essential is invisible to the eye."

You are my heart,

yiayia

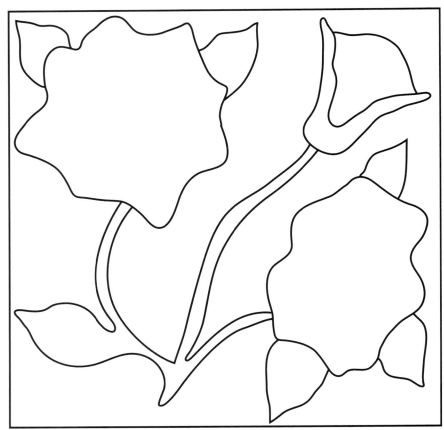

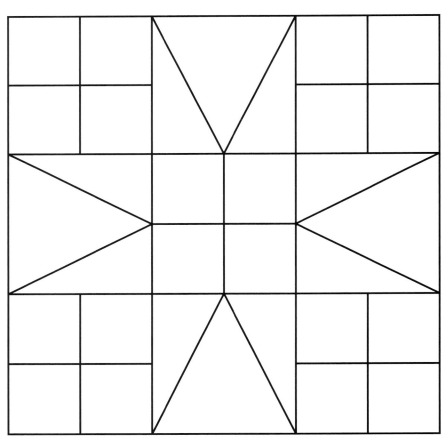

Dear Hannah: In the Style of Jane A. Stickle – Brenda Manges Papadakis

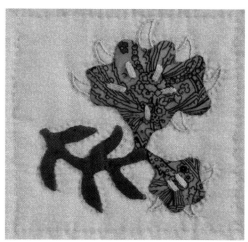

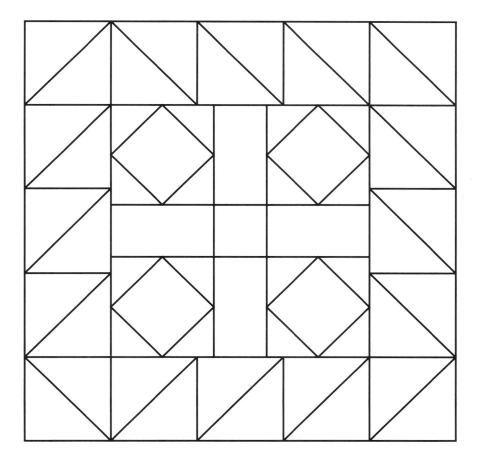

L-1
Sarah's Alley

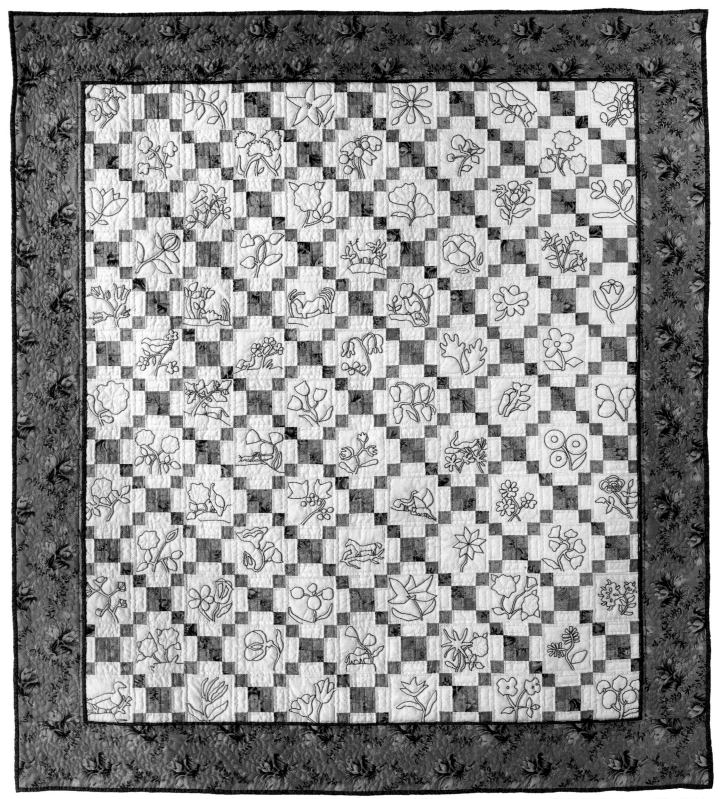

GRANDMA AND ME, 60" x 70". Redwork by Pam Austin, Temple City, California. Assembled by Kathleen Springer, Westfield, Indiana. Hand-quilted by Amish friends in Pennsylvania. Collection of the author.

Dear Hannah: In the Style of Jane A. Stickle – Brenda Manges Papadakis

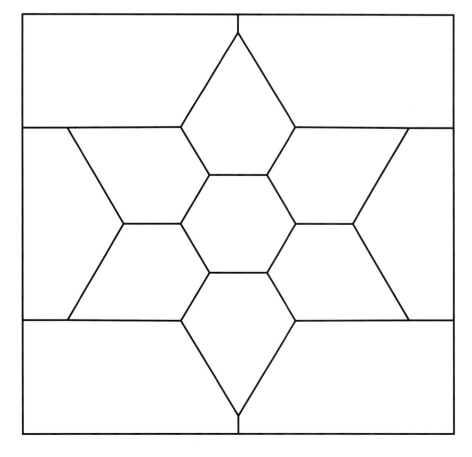

Dear Hannah: In the Style of Jane A. Stickle – Brenda Manges Papadakis

L-4
Queen Cotton

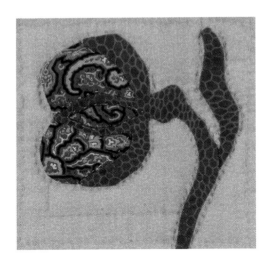

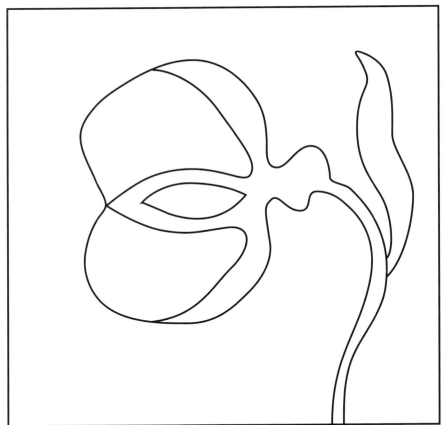

L-5
Ledge's State Park

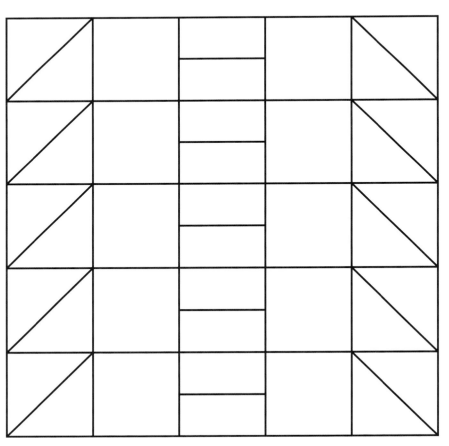

Dear Hannah: In the Style of Jane A. Stickle – Brenda Manges Papadakis

This is our cry. This is our prayer.
Peace in the world.
—Base of the Children's Monument,
Hiroshima Park, Japan

Beloved Hannah,

When I visited the Hiroshima Memorial Peace Park in June 1994, I sat beside a woman who spoke no English. Yet we "talked" for almost an hour! She was a schoolgirl when Hiroshima was bombed. She told me about running out of the school with her little dress on fire, and she relayed to me other horrors for her and the other children. Along with her heart, her pretty face was scarred, as were the remains of the buildings. We hugged each other and cried for all those whose lives were lost, and then we parted company.

The day turned joyous as I toured the Peace Park grounds. Every monument and fence was filled with chains of origami paper cranes. These cranes are a reminder of Sadako, a little girl born during World War II. She developed cancer as a result of atomic fallout. Sadako made paper cranes during her illness. She fell short of her goal of 1,000 paper cranes before she passed away. There is a monument to her in Hiroshima Park and children still make paper cranes in her memory. You have a flower for Sadako (K–7) in your quilt, and we will read her story together.

The Peace Park was filled with laughing and playing school children on their annual holiday. Several groups ran up to me to have their pictures taken. Oh, Hannah, how they giggled knowing I understood their English!

Another schoolgirl of World War II was Anne Frank. Anne and Her family moved to Amsterdam in 1933 because of the German oppression of the Jews. Anne was 4 years old, just about your age, Hannah. By 1940, the Germans had occupied Holland. On June 12, 1942, Anne received a diary for her thirteenth birthday. Soon afterward, the family moved into the attic of their business in Amsterdam. Anne wrote in her diary until August 4, 1944. The family was betrayed. Anne and seven others were arrested and taken to concentration camps. Anne died of typhus in 1945. Her father was the only member of her family to survive, and he published *The Diary of Anne Frank* in 1947. While she told of the horrors of the War, she also revealed her inner self, her ideals, and her desire "to go on living even after my death." Anne showed us that the story of oneself is really all we have in this life. Hannah, the Dutch Mill block (H–9) in your quilt is a tribute to Anne and all of the other children in the war.

Are you keeping a diary?

yiayia

L-6
Foxy Lady

L-7
Babe

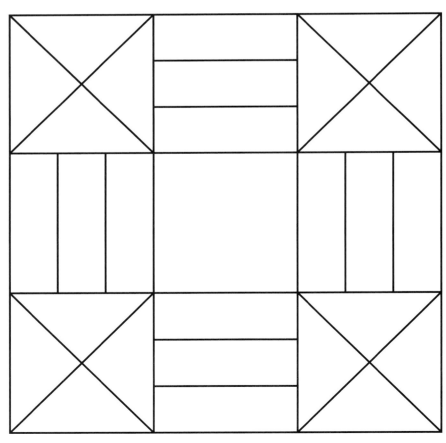

Dear Hannah: In the Style of Jane A. Stickle – Brenda Manges Papadakis

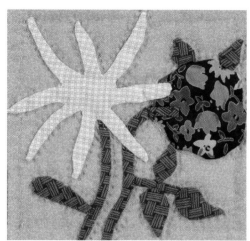

Dear Hannah: In the Style of Jane A. Stickle – Brenda Manges Papadakis

*This I believe with all my heart. If we want a free
and peaceful world – we can do it!*
—Eleanor Roosevelt

Dear Hannah,

Your grandmother is in Vermont celebrating Jane Stickle and her quilt. Many friendships have been formed on the Internet, and some of these friends are meeting each other face-to-face for the first time. It is hard to contain my excitement!

The end of the 1940s was a pleasant time, Hannah. The microwave was invented, and the first MacDonald's was opened. It's difficult to imagine our lives without these two milestones. The Universal Declaration of Human Rights was written in an effort to see that people all over the world were treated with respect and dignity. Eleanor Roosevelt was one of the writers of this declaration.

Ah, the women.... In spite of being declared citizens, having the right to vote, and earning their own money, women were still struggling for equal rights. Women were having trouble finding jobs after the war, and there was always the worry about childcare. Many men would have women stay home and "tend to their knitting and their children."

Women were knitting, Hannah, and they were also quilting. Right through the Great Depression and World War II, women continued to make quilts. However, there was a decline in the number of quiltmakers during the war. Many of the quilts during this time had a patriotic theme with red, white, and blue.

One of the quilters from this time was Grace McCance Snyder. She seemed determined to set a record for the number of pieces in a quilt. Mrs. Snyder sewed 87,789 tiny triangles together to make FLOWER BASKET PETIT POINT. This quilt was chosen by *Quilter's Newsletter Magazine* as one of the best quilts of the twentieth century. I know how much you like numbers, Hannah, so you have a block in your quilt with ninety-five pieces! It is Which Way to Oz (F–9).

You're my little quilter,

yiayia

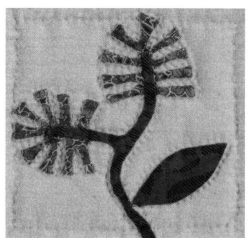

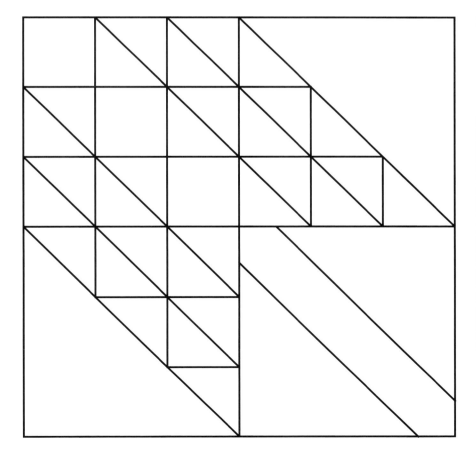

M–1
Mallard Crossing

M–2
Flying Bats

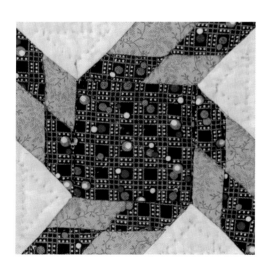

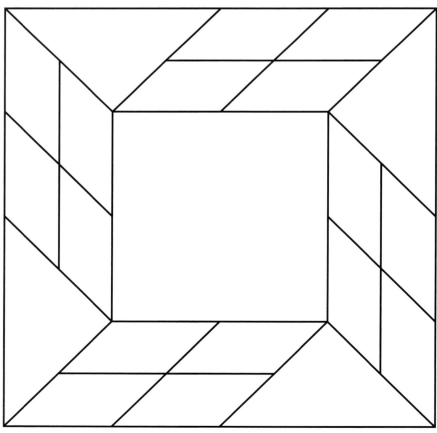

Dear Hannah: In the Style of Jane A. Stickle – Brenda Manges Papadakis

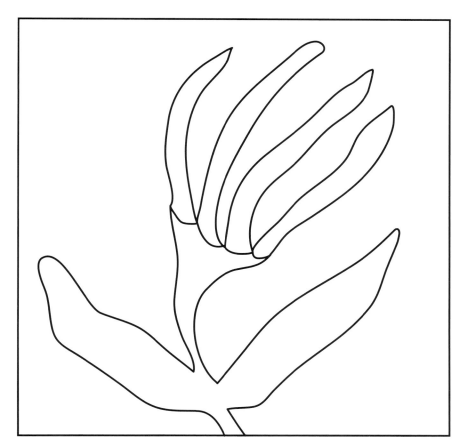

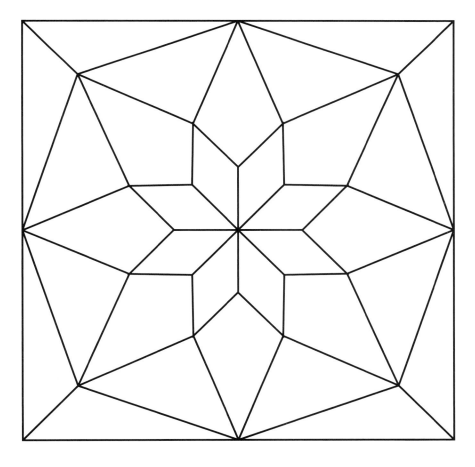

M–4
Pole Star

Dear Hannah: In the Style of Jane A. Stickle – Brenda Manges Papadakis

All I really need is love, but a little chocolate now and then doesn't hurt!

—Lucy Van Pelt

So, Baby Girl,

You and I are in Opryland at your first quilt show. You think it's Cinderella's ball! You dyed a bit of fabric, selected a big blue button for your collection, and bought your very first silver thimble. The only thing you find better than all of these things is sleeping under Yiayia's SPIRIT OF JANE STICKLE quilt. I tell you how very special it is, that it was made by more than two-hundred people and given to me in Vermont. Then you say, "Two-hundred? Yiayia, are you sure it wasn't just one-hundred?"

Then you want me to make you one in pink! Thinking about pink takes me back to the 50s. Yiayia and her friends were playing kick-the-can and hide-and-seek. Color television became available, and children everywhere watched the Mickey Mouse Club and Howdy Doody. Charles Schultz created the Peanuts cartoon with Snoopy and all his friends. Bill Haley and the Comets rocked us Around the Clock. The world was great for young girls in ponytails and pink poodle skirts. The 50s offered something special for people of all ages.

On a more serious note, the first commercial digital computer, UNIVAC, was installed in Philadelphia. The Atomic Energy Commission produced the first electricity from a nuclear reactor. DNA was discovered and the mystery of life revealed.

What was happening in the quilt world? Most "modern" women weren't really interested in quiltmaking. Your Gran said to me, "Why would I make an old quilt when I can buy a new blanket?" There were others, Hannah, like Charlotte Jane Whitehall and Rose G. Kretsinger, who were making wonderful appliquéd quilts.

There were fabrics with large prints of flowers and vegetables available for making tablecloths, curtains, and aprons. Many Western American prints were also popular during this time: cowboys and hats, and desert scenes with wagons and cacti. Fabrics also included ribbons, polka dots, printed plaids, and checks, as well as Mickey Mouse and Little Orphan Annie. We must study some of these fabrics in my stash, Little One.

You're my Cinderella!

yiayia

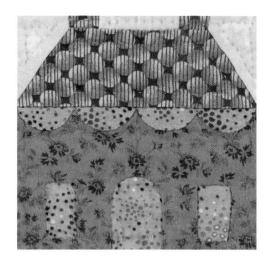

M–8
Columbia

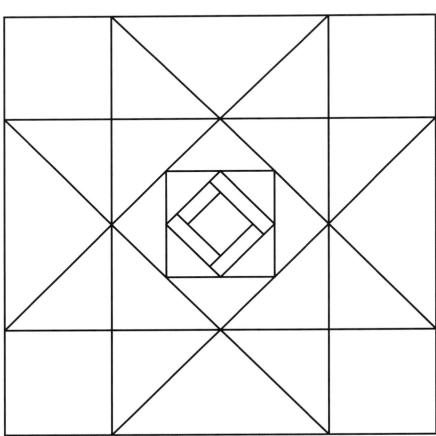

Dear Hannah: In the Style of Jane A. Stickle – Brenda Manges Papadakis

BATON ROUGE, LA 70801
PM
30 MAR
2001

Common sense is seeing things as they are; and doing things as they ought to be.
—Harriet Beecher Stowe

Precious Hannah,

When Yiayia was a little girl, every time I left to go swimming, my mother had this anxious look on her face. It was fear of polio. In school, we saved dimes for the March of Dimes to help polio victims. In 1955, Jonas Salk discovered the polio vaccine, and we took it in a sugar cube. Thank God, this will never be a concern for you, Angel.

The 50s were also a time for "separate but equal" facilities in our country. On December 1, 1955, Mrs. Rosa Parks sat down in the bus, exhausted from a day's work as a seamstress. Mrs. Parks was well-educated and a long–time NAACP worker. When she was asked to give up her seat for a white man, Mrs. Parks refused. She was arrested and taken to jail. This incident stimulated The Montgomery Bus Boycott and a ten-year struggle for freedom and justice. So you see, my Precious, even though the Amendments are in the Constitution, the country's opinions may not change overnight.

While the Civil Rights Movement continued, the singing sensation from Memphis, Elvis Presley, appeared on the Ed Sullivan Show. Girls all over the country fell instantly in love with him. Russia launched Sputnik II and the Space Race began. Alaska and Hawaii become our forty-ninth and fiftieth states.

Quilters were using patterns similar to some of those in your quilt, Hannah, although they weren't unique to the 50s. One of these block patterns is the Pinwheel (D–9). Two more blocks are Flying Bats (M–2) and Pickle Dish (I–4).

And what were the children doing? The very same thing my Hannah is doing now: playing with the brand new Barbie doll! Hoola hoops were also a new toy in the 50s. The teens were rock 'n rolling on American Bandstand, and families were going to drive-in movies.

You're my Barbie,

yiayia

M–9
Lucy & Katy

M–10
Katie's Pinwheel

Dear Hannah: In the Style of Jane A. Stickle – Brenda Manges Papadakis

BONUS BLOCK
Cracker

In EUROPEAN JANE, page 93.

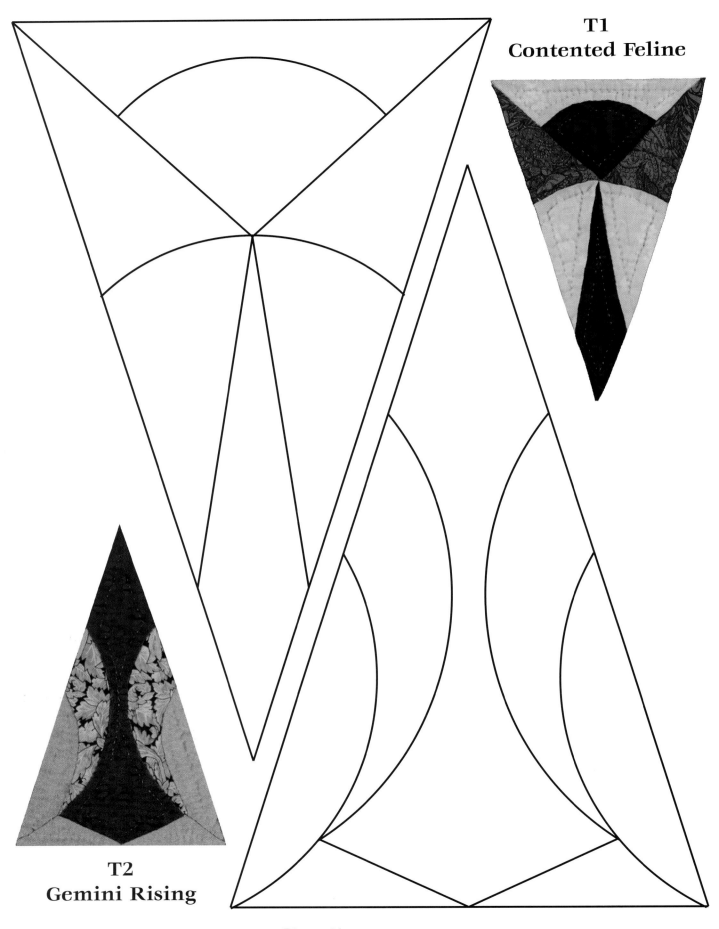

**T1
Contented Feline**

**T2
Gemini Rising**

Dear Hannah: In the Style of Jane A. Stickle – Brenda Manges Papadakis

BURBANK, CA 91501
PM
27 JUL
2001

There are some things you learn best in calm, and some in storm.

—Willa Cather

Dear Sweet Hannah,

What a trip! Yiayia is in California for the taping of "Simply Quilts" with Alex Anderson. Thank goodness my friend, Leah Estrin, was with me to keep my feet on the ground!

A few weeks ago, you came to Yiayia's for your first quilt retreat. We sewed and ate and played with our Shipshewana friends. You really struggled to make a four patch on the Featherweight. When I asked how you liked sewing on the machine, you rubbed your little forehead and said, "I like it better when I just sew with a needle and thread and go up and down in the favric." Oh, how you love your favric!

And the 60s was a time for fabric, Hannah! We had polyester, in solids and in big prints. There were supergraphic fabrics in bold and bright colors. There were also psychedelic and watercolor-looking fabrics. We also had fabrics with jewel tones and florals.

"Flower Power" became the big phrase during the 60s. The hippies came out in their sandals, bell-bottom pants, and floral dresses telling everyone to "turn on, tune in, and drop out." Many people protested America's being in the Vietnam War, which Papou says was one of the biggest mistakes in our country's history. The motto "make love, not war" became popular, as did a movement to go "back to nature."

As part of this movement, a revival of all things handcrafted took place. Yes, baby girl, there was quilting! Women continued to quilt in rural areas. For most of the nation, there was a renewed interest in the quilts made by our grandmothers. There was also the voices of quilt artists like Jean Ray Laury. Her quilts were unconventional with sometimes a political or humorous theme. Bonnie Leman is another voice of the quilt revival. She started *Quilter's Newsletter Magazine* in 1969 from her kitchen table. It is still in publication today, Hannah.

I love you!

yiayia

**T3
Sands of Time**

**T4
Alpha's Prayer**

Dear Hannah: In the Style of Jane A. Stickle – Brenda Manges Papadakis

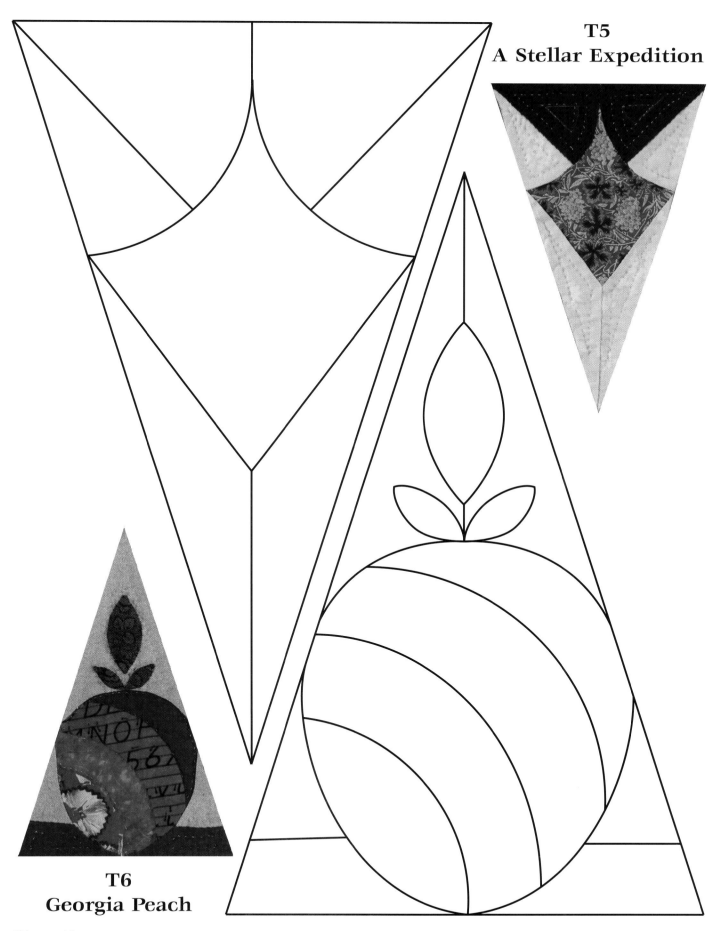

T5
A Stellar Expedition

T6
Georgia Peach

**T7
Peering Through
the Keyhole**

**T8
The Bishop's Halo**

Dear Hannah: In the Style of Jane A. Stickle – Brenda Manges Papadakis

**T9
Alcoa Tornadoes**

**T10
Through the
Needle's Eye**

TEATIME WITH HANNAH, 40¾" x 37". By Mary Althaus, Whitewater, Wisconsin and Naples, Florida.

Hooked rug, 32" x 32". By Sandra Kandris, Des Moines, Iowa.

Dear Hannah: In the Style of Jane A. Stickle – Brenda Manges Papadakis

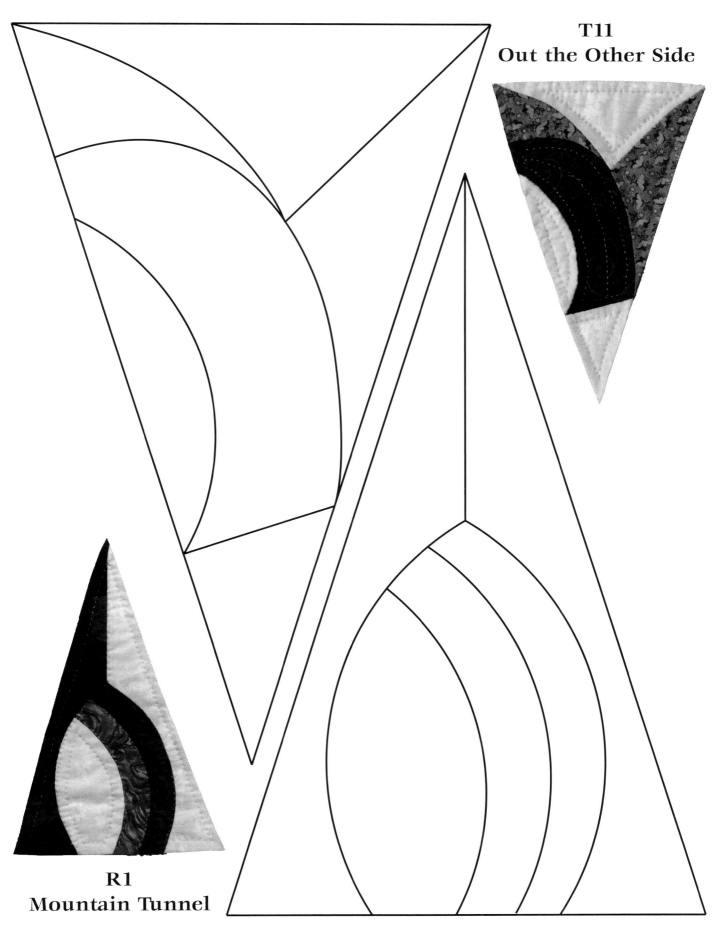

**T11
Out the Other Side**

**R1
Mountain Tunnel**

**R2
Primrose Path**

**R3
Curtain Call**

Dear Hannah: In the Style of Jane A. Stickle – Brenda Manges Papadakis

Americans will always remember what happened on September 11. We cannot ease the pain, but we can redouble our efforts to ensure that our lives have meaning and that liberty and justice prevail.

First Lady Laura Bush

Oh, dearest Hannah,

How do I tell an innocent little girl about the horrors of September 11? Two planes flew into the Twin Towers, one flew into the Pentagon, and one crashed in a Pennsylvania field. Several thousand people lost their lives in these senseless terrorist acts. I can hardly talk about it, Little One. All I want to do is cry and pray. It seems like a very bad movie. My friend Gail and I decided to go on with our trip to New Jersey and Long Island. You cannot let fear paralyze you, Hannah. You must continue to be free to go where you want to go.

I am so glad Gail is with me. We went to Vickie Fallon's and celebrated life and birthdays! Yiayia is lucky to have such dear friends. Then we went on to Long Island, passing right by Ground Zero. The Statue of Liberty, with her torch held high for all to see, never had such meaning to Yiayia as now. Indeed, there is a block in your quilt that represents our freedom, Lady Liberty (F-11). She has seven spokes in her crown, representing the seven continents of the world.

Almost a month ago, Yiayia was in Oklahoma City. I visited the memorial where another terrorist had bombed an office building. One hundred sixty-eight people lost their lives. As we sat at the Memorial, a soft breeze came across the water from the little seats representing the victims. I believe it was their spirits reaching out to comfort those of us who were there. It was a very tender, beautiful moment in my life. At the entrance to the Memorial is the following statement, "We come here to remember those who were killed, those who survived, and those lives are changed forever. May all who leave here know the impact of violence. May this memorial offer comfort, strength, peace, hope and serenity."

Beloved, Hannah, my experience in Oklahoma gives me comfort today. I want to be with you and hold you closely. I do have joy in my heart thinking about your singing "God Bless America" at the top of your precious voice.

And may God bless you,

yiayia

**R4
Northern Neck Water**

**R5
Aladdin's Door**

Dear Hannah: In the Style of Jane A. Stickle – Brenda Manges Papadakis

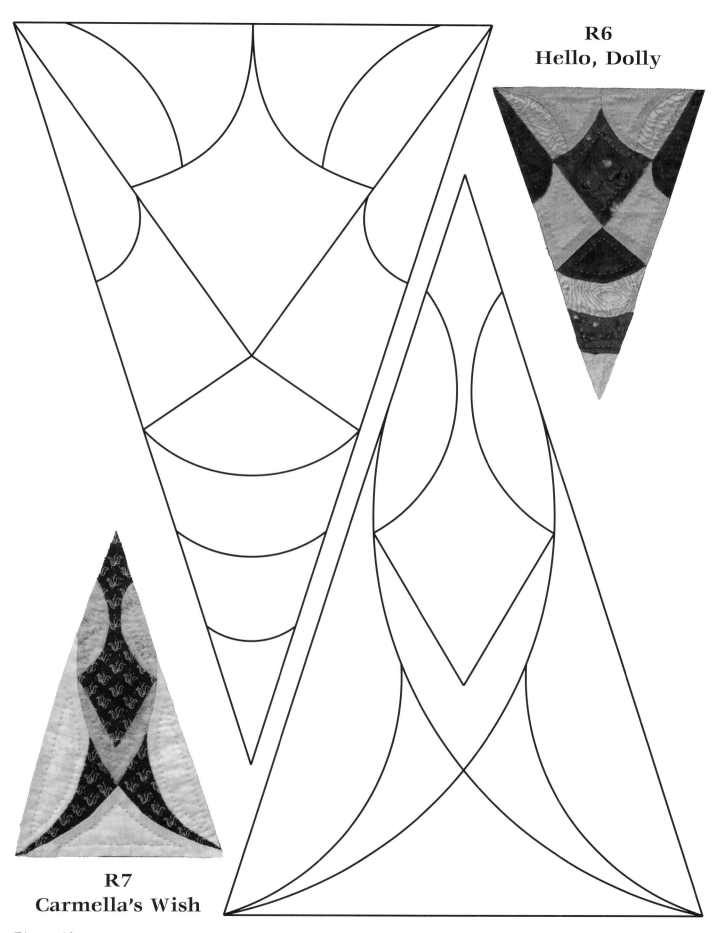

**R6
Hello, Dolly**

**R7
Carmella's Wish**

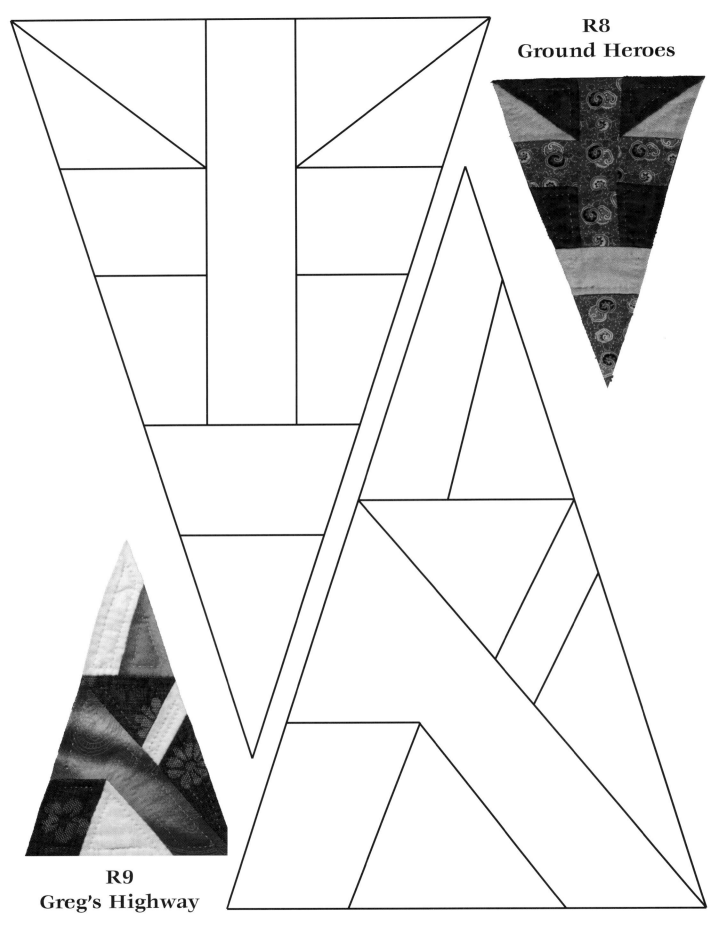

**R8
Ground Heroes**

**R9
Greg's Highway**

Dear Hannah: In the Style of Jane A. Stickle – Brenda Manges Papadakis

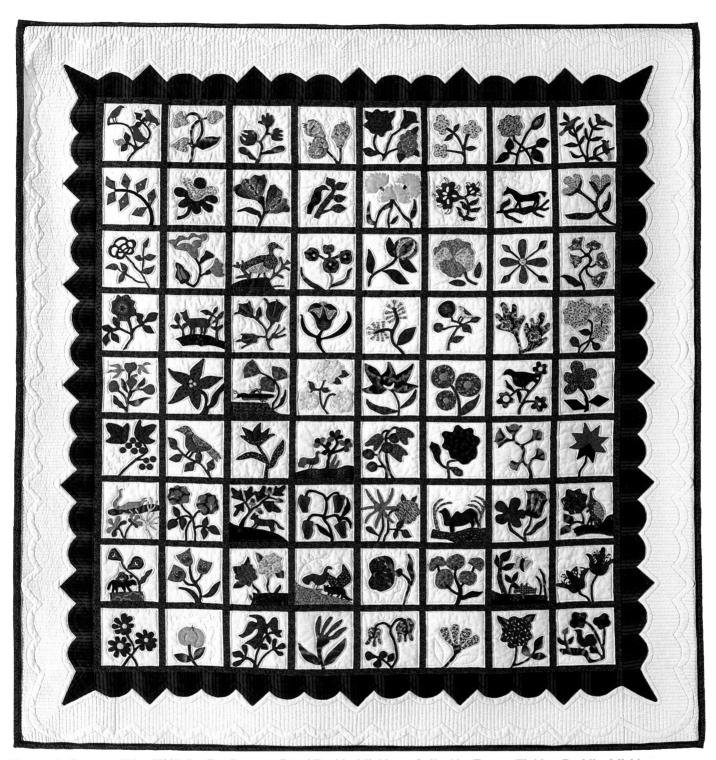

HANNAH'S GARDEN, 51" x 55½". By Gay Bomers, Grand Rapids, Michigan. Quilted by Tammy Finkler, Conklin, Michigan.

**R10
Pyramid of Hope**

**R-11
Fort Antes
Memorial**

Dear Hannah: In the Style of Jane A. Stickle – Brenda Manges Papadakis

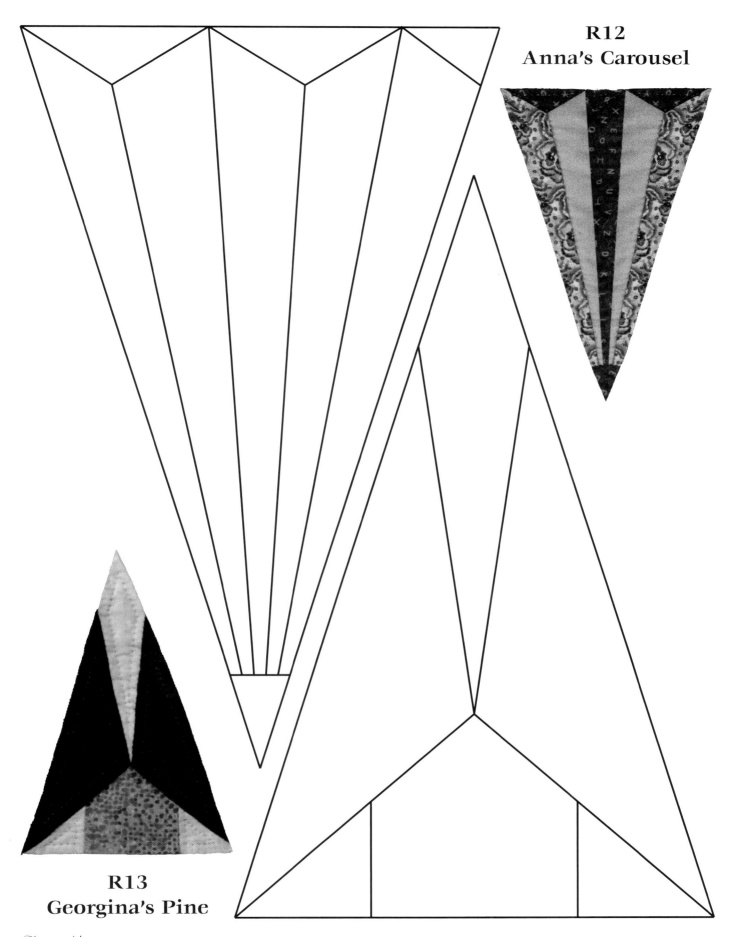

**R12
Anna's Carousel**

**R13
Georgina's Pine**

**B11
Topsy Turvey**

**B10
Bunker Hill**

Dear Hannah: In the Style of Jane A. Stickle – Brenda Manges Papadakis

May the creations of my hands reflect the contents of my heart.
—Dana Shanes Lynch

Ah, dear Hannah,

In a few days, you will be six years old! You were anxious about starting kinder-garten, and now your mom can't keep you away. Soon, you will be able to travel long distances with me. What fun! My friend Virginia and I are in Dover, and I'm thinking about you tonight. Once again, it is the quilters sharing friendship that makes everything so wonderful. When we arrived in Dover, there was a Dear Jane party and special show—and—tell. There was even a cake decorated with Jane Blocks! Little One, everyone everywhere seems more open and more gentle since September 11. The hugs are closer, and the laughter and the tears flow more freely.

There were some serious events in the 60s too, Hannah. Our youngest President, John Kennedy, was inaugurated in 1961. He was assassinated in 1963. We were in a space race with Russia to land a man on the moon. The Soviets put the first women in space. In 1964, President Johnson signed the Civil Rights Act. One lady who got everyone's attention was biologist Rachel Carson. She told us of the damage we were doing to our environment and the harm that would come if we continued this practice. Her book, *Silent Spring*, made us aware of the need to protect our environment.

On a lighter note, the Beatles and Elvis Presley were entertaining people all over the world with their music during the 60s. In 1969, a big rock concert was held in Woodstock, New York. There were 500,000 people. As the 60s drew to a close, Neil Armstrong walked on the moon, saying, "That's one small step for man, one giant leap for mankind." Your Yiayia was stepping and leaping all right, with your mom and Uncle Michael to the all-new Sesame Street band!

I'll march in your band!

yiayia

**B9
Thelma's Bloom**

**B8
Points, Lines, Planes**

Dear Hannah: In the Style of Jane A. Stickle – Brenda Manges Papadakis

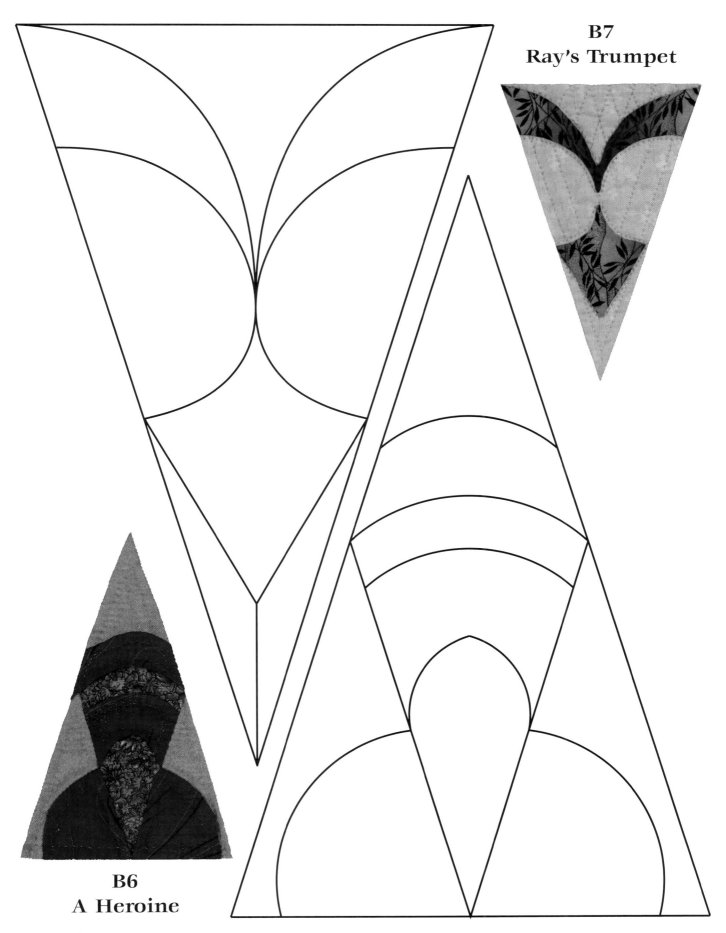

**B7
Ray's Trumpet**

**B6
A Heroine**

INDIANAPOLIS, IN 46207
PM
31 DEC
2001

I myself have never been able to find out precisely what feminism is; I only know that people call me a feminist whenever I express sentiments that differentiate me from a doormat.

—Rebecca West

Dearest Hannah,

You are having a grand time in kindergarten. You love to move to the different learning stations, especially your favorite, math. Your stories remind me of your mommy in kindergarten. At that time, a new Women's Liberation Movement began. The Civil Rights movement inspired women to demand their equal place in society. You know, Sweetheart, this is just history repeating itself. I think perhaps there will always be some conflict with women and equality. I wonder what issues will concern you.

One big issue of the 70s was the Roe vs. Wade case. The Supreme Court guaranteed woman's choice in 1973. Another landmark for women was the passage of Title IX. Federal money must be divided equally between male and female sports programs.

In 1973, Billy Jean King defeated Bobby Riggs in the tennis Battle of the Sexes. Ms. Riggs said that she was trying to push the women's movement forward at a time when women couldn't even get their own credit cards.

To be honest with you, Hannah, my life in the 70s was my babies. I didn't really have time to be active in the women's movement. Uncle Jason was born in 1971, and your mom and Uncle Michael were in kindergarten and first grade. I received my teaching degree, and a divorce, in 1972. I finished graduate school in 1976, and also made her first quilt that year.

In 1971, Disney World opened in Orlando, Florida, for the pleasure of children. In New York, Jonathan Holstein and Gail Van Der Hoof hung an exhibit of quilts for the joy of women. The exhibit was called "Abstract Design in American Quilts," and it was held at the Whitney Museum. These quilts alone seem to have stirred the passion and souls of women. After the Whitney Museum, the exhibit traveled all over the world <u>for four years</u>.Thus began the "The Great Quilt Revival." America was nearing its Bicentennial, and just as in the 1870s, quiltmaking played a big role in the celebrations.

I celebrate you!

yiayia

B5
Beyond the Horizon

B4
Cardinal Rule

**B3
Angel Song**

**B2
A-skewed**

Dear Hannah: In the Style of Jane A. Stickle – Brenda Manges Papadakis

**B1
Rise of the Pyramid**

**L13
Teepee**

BASKETS FOR HANNAH, 43" x 56". By Gail Stewart, Naples, Florida and Overland Park, Kansas

FLYING GEESE FOR BRENDA, 18½" x 18½". By Jennifer Perkins, Harlan, Iowa.

Dear Hannah: In the Style of Jane A. Stickle – Brenda Manges Papadakis

**L12
Obediah's Odyssey**

**L11
The Cardinal**

**L10
Swimming Upstream**

**L9
Silent Wisdom**

Dear Hannah: In the Style of Jane A. Stickle – Brenda Manges Papadakis

You can do what I cannot do. I can do what you cannot do. Together we can do beautiful things for God.
—Mother Teresa

Dear Baby Girl,

Child, you are adorable, with that big grin and two missing teeth, singing "God Bless the USA!" You are one flag-waving, patriotic girl! Hannah, it is also important to love and care for others.

One person who is an example to us all is a nun, Mother Teresa. In 1979, Mother Teresa won the Nobel Peace Prize for her tireless work helping the poor in India. Today, she is being nominated for Sainthood. In fact, Little One, the 1980s created an awareness of the needs of the starving all over the world. Concerts and music marathons were held to raise money for food and medicine.

And what do you think your Yiayia was doing in the 80s? Dreaming about quilts! Jinny Beyer's Patchwork Patterns came out in 1979. Ms. Beyer wrote three more books in the next five years, each one rich in information and history. Yiayia tried to memorize every one of them!

Bruce Mann, a Kentucky quilt dealer, wanted the history of Kentucky quilts and their makers to be preserved. After he died, his friends carried out his dream. Quiltmakers Eleanor Bingham Miller and Shelly Zegart held documentation days all over the state. In 1982, selected quilts were exhibited in Louisville, and the book Kentucky Quilts 1800-1900 (The Kentucky Quilt Project, Inc., 1982) was published. This was the first State Quilt Project. Today, we have numerous books from many state projects. Michigan, California, and Rhode Island are a few of these books.

Hannah, we had other exciting events in the early 80s. Sandra Day O'Connor was sworn in as the first female Supreme Court Justice. Wilma Mankiller became the first female Principal Chief of the Cherokee nation. By the mid–80s, almost thirty percent of the doctoral degrees in the country were earned by women.

You're my little woman,

yiayia

L8
Leah's Fancy

L7
New Beginnings

Dear Hannah: In the Style of Jane A. Stickle – Brenda Manges Papadakis

L6
Bill & Nancy's Dream

L5
Ocean Music

Our future lies with today's kids and tomorrow's space exploration.

—Sally Ride

Precious Hannah,

Yiayia is having a grand time leafing through her magazines of the 80s. In fact, Jane Stickle's quilt is in one! What fun we will have looking at them when you're ready for me to tell you about the "olden days" of quilting.

Hannah, one teacher who was a great influence on quilting in the 80s was Elly Sienkiewicz. Her first book, *Spoken Without a Word*, was self-published in 1983. Elly introduced us to the Fascinating Ladies of Baltimore who created wondrous appliqué quilts from 1840–1850.

Another teacher at this time, Little One, was Mary Ellen Hopkins. Mary Ellen revolutionized quilting with a rotary cutter and mat and a multitude of fast-piecing tricks. Another influential teacher was Roberta Horton. Roberta taught us to use a variety of fabrics in designing our own quilts: plaids, stripes, big prints, African prints, and Japanese prints. All of these teachers are still very active, Hannah Lou, and it would be wonderful if you have a chance to take a class from them.

America in the mid–80s had about fourteen million people involved with quilts, according to quilt historian Jonathan Holstein. There were shows and shops with delights for everyone.

Hannah, the biggest delight for Yiayia at this time was the birth of your cousin Benjamin George on November 15, 1985. Oh, my, did I ever go spinning in circles! Seems like only yesterday Ben and I were painting whiskers on our faces to have a party with his kitty Nancy.

The 80s was also an eventful time for women in NASA'S space program. On June 18, 1983, Dr. Sally Ride became the first American woman in space aboard the Challenger. On January 28, 1986, Hannah, the space shuttle Challenger exploded after lift–off. It was a terrible tragedy for the nation. Two women were members of the flight crew, Judy Resnick and Christa McCauliffe. Christa was the first teacher in space. She always told her students to "Reach for the stars, I'll be there." The Challenger block (K–2) in your quilt is a tribute to these special women.

You're my little star,

yiayia

**L4
Little Church
in the Woods**

**L3
Autumn Leaves**

**L2
Sunrise**

**L1
Ascending Staircase**

Dear Hannah: In the Style of Jane A. Stickle – Brenda Manges Papadakis

DEAR ALLISON, 19¼" x 25½". By Karen L. Flanscha, Cedar Rapids, Iowa.

Aerodynamically, the bumblebee shouldn't be able to fly, but the bumblebee doesn't know it so it goes on flying anyway.

—Mary Kay Ash

Dear Hannah,

Here we are in Opryland at the American Quilter's Society show. What a special trip! Yiayia gets to play with you, Nathan, and her Dear Jane friends too. An added blessing was a visit with my childhood friend, Mimi. You will learn that being with an old friend provides the same comfort as curling up with a favorite quilt, Sweetheart.

And my beautiful granddaughter? She needs a larger silver thimble and another button bracelet. As we walk around the quilt show, Hannah, I think of the changes in quiltmaking in the last twenty years. One of the biggest friends to quilters is the computer. Some of the other techniques we have now are also relatively new: quick-piecing, rotary cutting, foundation piecing, and machine quilting.

Machine quilting isn't really new, Baby. Women have been machine quilting since Howe patented his sewing machine in 1846. In the mid-80s, Harriet Hargrave made machine quilting an art form. It took a while for machine quilting to be accepted. Opponents would say it wasn't a "real" quilt unless it was hand quilted. Now machine quilted quilts are prizewinners in shows all over the country.

Other prizewinners are art quilts. As early as the quilt revival of the 60s and 70s, Hannah, according to The *Art Quilt* magazine, artists were "moving quilts from beds to the walls." The flood gates opened and contemporary artists had a new medium. Yvonne Porcella said, "Therefore, getting beyond bed-size is good. It is forcing us to innovate." Once again, there was controversy. This time it was the traditional versus the contemporary quilt. Were contemporary quilts really quilts? Of course they were! Yiayia always studied the art quilts, Little One. The works of such artists as Michael James and Ruth McDowell fascinated me. One day, Hannah, it is important for you to try a variety of quiltmaking styles before choosing one as your own.

You're my art quilt!

yiayia

Dear Hannah: In the Style of Jane A. Stickle – Brenda Manges Papadakis

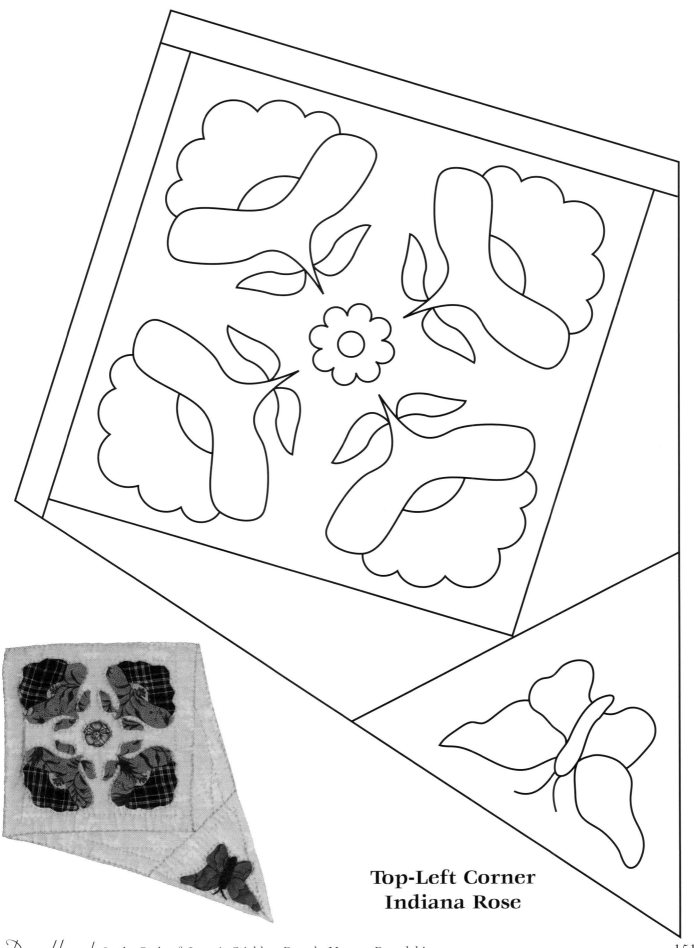

**Top-Left Corner
Indiana Rose**

**Top-Right Corner
Soldier's Compass**

Dear Hannah: In the Style of Jane A. Stickle – Brenda Manges Papadakis

BOWLING GREEN, OH 43402
PM
27 AUG
2002

Let our lives be in accordance with our convictions of Right, each striving to carry out our principles.

—Lucretia Mott

My Beloved Hannah,

You are now in the first grade. What a milestone! We will remember this event by the Texas Schoolhouse block (A–6) in your quilt. Yiayia is having a landmark time too. Electric Quilt Company is making a CD rom of *Dear Jane!* Jane Stickle and her quilt will now enjoy the very best of cyberspace. It has been twelve years since your Yiayia became obsessed with Jane Stickle and her quilt. I was awed by her designs, and my "sole" mission was to give Jane and her patterns to the world. What a dream come true!

Truly, Little One, the 90s was the decade for innovation in the computer world. As the technology grew, so did its use in the quilt world. Electric Quilt Company christened their first edition of EQ in 1991 on Penny McMorris's television show, "The Great American Quilt." Mr. Neumann's fascination with the geometric patterns in quilts led him to develop a program for people to use in designing their own quilts. You have three blocks from Electric Quilt in your quilt: Jacob's Compass (L–9), Pole Star (M–4), and Star & Crescent (K–4). Many of the other blocks were also drafted on the computer. It is certainly easier than using a compass and ruler!

Quilting is a spiraling industry now. There has been so much interest in old quilts and textiles that fabric companies started making reproductions of them. You'll find many of these reproductions in your quilt. There are so many new books, techniques, and teachers, Hannah, that your Yiayia has difficulty keeping up with them.

Women are making progress too, Baby Girl. The media called 1992 "The Year of the Woman," because of the number of female candidates for public office. In 1993, Janet Reno became the first female U.S. Attorney General.

One of the most influential women of the 90s was Oprah Winfrey. Since "The Oprah Winfrey Show" became nationwide in 1986, she has devoted her energy to helping others. Oprah also advocates that everyone keep a journal.

You're my biggest influence!

yiayia

Dear Hannah: In the Style of Jane A. Stickle – Brenda Manges Papadakis

Bottom-Right Corner
Oak Leaf & Reel

Remember our heritage is our power; we can know ourselves and our capacities by seeing that other women have been strong.
                                        —©Judy Chicago, 1979

Beloved Hannah Lou,

These past seven years with you have been an incredible journey. Snuggling and giggling at bedtime, unexpected kisses on a carousel horse, your little wave during a ballet recital — all of these wonderful memories are written in my heart.

Hannah, I have tried to present the reality of human mistakes and successes. I want you to know how much can be accomplished from just one person's dream and how powerful one creative idea can be. I want you to feel two centuries of women's struggle and a sense of pride for yourself, your country, and your heritage. These are your cornerstones.

Your life in the twenty-first century, Precious, will be so totally different from those whose stories you read here. It will also be unlike your Yiayia's. You must have information to fully enjoy life. I want you to study the past with one hand and relish the newness of change with the other.

You can place *Dear Hannah* in your "Life Suitcase" and carry it with you when you travel. In your youth, you must rely on the wisdom of adults who love you to guide you and help fill your Suitcase. Your family and other trusted people will never lie to you because you are precious to them.

As you cross over into adulthood, you will be making your own decisions. It will then be time to evaluate all of the items in your Suitcase. Those things that are honest and useful to you should remain with you. The items that are out-dated and inappropriate for your life should be thrown away.

Baby Girl, the world is becoming smaller and smaller. By the time you evaluate the contents of your Suitcase, the world will be like a little neighborhood. Travel with confidence and security and keep a journal of your story. Hannah, remember Yiayia is always with you, even when you can't see me. I am in your heart, for that's where Love is stored.

Oh, how I do love you!

yiayia

Bibliography

Beyer, Jinny. *Patchwork Patterns*. McLean, Virginia: EPM Publications, Inc., 1979.

Brackman, Barbara. *Encyclopedia of Pieced Quilt Patterns*. Paducah, Kentucky: AQS, 1993.

Clarke, Mary Washington. *Kentucky Quilts and Their Makers*. Lexington, Kentucky: University Press of Kentucky, 1976.

Cleveland, Richard, and Donna Bister. *Plain and Fancy*. Gualala, California: Quilt Digest Press, 1991.

Coleman, Penny. *Girls: a History of Growing Up Female in America*. New York: Scholastic, Inc., 2000.

Craig, Sharyn, and Harriet Hargrave. *The Art of Classic Quiltmaking*. Lafayette, California: C&T Publishing, 2000.

Duke, Dennis, and Deborah Harding. *America's Glorious Quilts*. New York: Crown Publishers, 1987.

Finley, John, and Jonathan Holstein. *Kentucky Quilts 1800–1900*. Louisville, Kentucky: The Kentucky Quilt Project, Inc., 1982.

Hall, Carrie A and Kretsinger, Rose, G. *The Romance of the Patchwork Quilt in America*. New York: Bonanza Books, 1935.

Hall, Eliza Calvert. *Aunt Jane of Kentucky*. Boston, Massachusetts: Little, Brown and Company, 1907.

Hargrave, Harriet. *From Fiber to Fabric*. Lafayette, California: C&T Publishing, 1997.

———. *Heirloom Machine Quilting*. Lafayette, California: C&T Publishing, 1990.

Holstein, Jonathan. *Abstract Design in American Quilts: A Biography of an Exhibition*. Louisville, Kentucky: The Kentucky Quilt Project, 1991.

Holstein, Jonathan, and John Finley. *Kentucky Quilts 1800–1900*. New York, NY: Random House, Pantheon Books, 1982.

Hopkins, Mary Ellen. *The It's Okay if You Sit on my Quilt Book*. Santa Monica, California: ME Publications, 1989.

Hopkinson, Bridget, and Miranda Smith, editors. *Children's History of the 20th Century*. New York: DK Publishing, Inc., 1999.

Horton, Laurel, editor. *Quiltmaking in America, Selected Writings by the American Quilt Study Group*. Nashville, Tennessee: Rutledge Hill Press, 1994.

Horton, Roberta. *An Amish Adventure: a Workbook for Color*. Lafayette, California: C&T Publishing, 1983.

Horton, Roberta. *Calico and Beyond: The Use of Patterned Fabric in Quilts*. Lafayette, California: C&T Publishing, 1986.

Kile, Michael, and Penny McMorris. *The Art Quilt*. San Francisco, California: Quilt Digest Press, 1986.

Kiracofe, Roderick. *The American Quilt*. New York: Clarkson N. Potter, Inc., 1993.

Larkin, Jack, and Bassett Z. Lynne. *Northern Comfort New England's Early Quilts 1780–1850*. Nashville, Tennessee: Rutledge Hill Press, 1998.

Laury, Jean Ray. *Appliqué Stitchery*. New York: Van Nostrandt Reinhold Company, 1966.

Lunardini, Christine. *What Every American Should Know About Women's History*. Holbrook, Massachusetts: Bab Adams, Inc., 1994.

Pottinger, David. *Quilts from the Indiana Amish*. New York: E.P. Dutton, Inc., 1983.

Ramsey, Bets, and Merikay Waldvogel. *Southern Quilts Surviving Relics of the Civil War*. Nashville, Tennessee: Rutledge Hill Press, 1998.

Sienkiewicz, Elly. *Baltimore Beauties and Beyond, Volume I*. Lafayette, California: C&T Publishing, 1989.

Sienkiewicz, Elly. *Spoken without a Word*. Washington, D.C.: Turtle Hill Press, 1983.

Waldvogel, Merikay. *Soft Covers for Hard Times: Quiltmaking in the Great Depression*. Nashville, Tennessee: Rutledge Hill Press, 1990.

Woodard, Thomas. K., and Blanche Greenstein, *Twentieth Century Quilts 1900–1950*. New York: E.P. Dutton, 1988.

Websites
britannica.com
dearjane.com
electricquilt.com
greatwomen.org
law.cornell.edu/constitution/
    constitution.table.html#amendments
law.emory.edu/FEDERAL/usconst.html
msn.ancestry.com/library/view/news/articles 6376.asp
pbs.org/onewoman/suffrage.html

pbs.org/onewoman/suffrage.html#ratification
pbs.org/onewoman/suffrage.html#strategies
quiltersbee.com/qbqhisto.htm#YR_1971
quiltershalloffame.org/Honorees/hotlstein.htm
quiltstudy.unl.edu/Press/98News/98_03.html
rbvhs.vusd.k12.ca.us
reddawn.net/quilt/timeline.htm
sadako.org/sadakostory.htm
scholastic.com
shellyquilts.com/KYQuilts_RootsandWings.html
time.com/time/time100/heroes/profile
time.com/time/time100/leaders/profile/eleanor4.html
tntech.edu/women/attune/fall02/
u.arizona.edu/~kari/rosie.htm
userpages.aug.com/captbarb/femvets4.html
vintagecars.about.com/library/weekly/aa072801a.htm
watson.org/~lisa/blackhistory/citing.html
whitehouse.gov/history/firstladies/ar32.html
womenofthewest.org/exhibits/suffrage/suffrage_wy.html
womenshistory.about.com/library/weekly/
    aa010329b.htm
womensrightsforever.org/amendment.html
wpafb.af.mil/museum/history/vietnam/prolog.htm

Quotations

Page 16, Cherokee proverb

Page 22, quote by First Lady Barbara Bush (1925–).

Page 25, quote by Susan B. Anthony (1820–1906), co-founder of the National Woman Suffrage Association.

Page 28, quote by French suffragette Hubertine Auclert (1848–1914).

Page 32, quote by Gerda Lerner (1920–), Women's History Reclamation Project. Permission granted by Gerda Lerner.

Page 42, quote by Martha Washington (1731–1802).

Page 47, quote by Aunt Jane of Kentucky, from *Aunt Jane of Kentucky*, by Eliza Calvert Obenchain, pen name Eliza Calvert Hall (1856–1935). Originally published in 1907. Reprint edition, University Press of Kentucky, March 1995.

Page 50, quote by Helen Keller (1880–1968), from *The Story of My Life* (1902).

Page 57, quote (1913) by Carrie Chapman Catt (1859–1947), an organizer for the International Woman Suffrage Association.

Page 63, quote by Charlotte Brontë (1816–1855), author of *Jane Eyre* .

Page 67, quote by Christine de Pisan (1364–1431), French poet and philosopher.

Page 77, quote by Marie Curie (1867–1934), French scientist, who with her husband, Pierre, discovered radium and polonium. Madame Curie was awarded the Nobel Prize for Chemistry in 1911.

Page 85, quote by U.S. aviator Amelia Mary Earhart (1897–1937), from an article in the *New York Times*, July 29, 1928.

Page 89, quote by U.S. astronomer Maria Mitchell (1818–1884).

Page 97, in Rosie the Riveter Park, Richmond, California.

Page 103, quote from base of the Children's Monument, Hiroshima Park, Japan.

Page 106, quote by Eleanor Roosevelt (1884–1962).

Page 110, quote by Lucy Van Pelt, from "Peanuts" cartoon by Charles M. Schulz. Permission granted by licensing coordinator United Media.

Page 113, quote by Harriet Beecher Stowe (1811–1896), author of *Uncle Tom's Cabin*.

Page 117, quote by U.S. novelist Willa Cather (1876–1947), from *The Song of the Lark* (1915).

Page 125, quote by First Lady Laura Bush (1946–).

Page 133, quote by Dana Shanes Lynch, friend of the author.

Page 136, quote by Rebecca West (1892–1983), from *The Clarion*, England (1913).

Page 143, quote by Mother Teresa (1910–1997), from her message to the Fourth U.N. Women's Conference.

Page 146, quote by astronaut Sally K. Ride (1951–). Permission granted by Dr. Sally K. Ride.

Page 150, quote by Mary Kay Ash (1915–2001), from *From My Heart*, self-published. Founder of Mary kay Cosmetics. Permission granted by her corporation.

Page 153, quote by women's advocate Lucretia Mott (1793–1880).

Page 156, quote by Judy Chicago (1939–), from © *The Dinner Party*, 1979. Permission granted by the artist's arts organization, Through the Flower.

About the Author

Brenda Papadakis, who has been making quilts since 1975, especially enjoys drafting and designing. She saw a photo of Jane Stickle's 1863 quilt and became so enamored that she spent the next five years researching the life and times in which Jane lived. The book *Dear Jane* is the result of that labor.

In 1997, Brenda retired, after teaching math for 25 years, to devote her time to lecturing and teaching, throughout the United States, Japan, and Holland, about Jane Stickle, the Civil War, and nineteenth century history. Articles about the Dear Jane phenomenon have appeared in *McCall's Vintage Quilt Magazine*, *Ladies Circle Patchwork Quilts*, as well as quilting magazines in Holland, Australia, and Denmark and Japan.

Other AQS Books

This is only a small selection of the books available from the American Quilter's Society. AQS books are known worldwide for timely topics, clear writing, beautiful color photos, and accurate illustrations and patterns. The following books are available from your local bookseller, quilt shop, or public library.

#6399 CD-ROM   us$24.95

#5019   us$25.95

#6403 CD-ROM   us$49.95

#6009   us$19.95

#6300   us$24.95

#6293   us$24.95

#6208   us$24.95

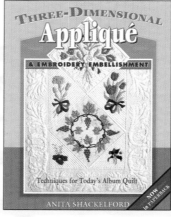

#6292   us$24.95

#6007   us$22.95

LOOK for these books nationally, **CALL** or **VISIT** our website at www.AQSquilt.com

1-800-626-5420